Better Homes and Gardens®

Summertime Cooking

Our seal assures you that every recipe in *Summertime Cooking*
has been tested in the Better Homes and Gardens® Test Kitchen.
This means that each recipe is practical and reliable,
and meets our high standards of taste appeal.

BETTER HOMES AND GARDENS® BOOKS

Editor: Gerald M. Knox
Art Director: Ernest Shelton
Managing Editor: David A. Kirchner
Project Editors: James D. Blume, Marsha Jahns
Project Managers: Liz Anderson, Jennifer Speer Ramundt,
    Angela Renkoski

Editor, Food and Family Life: Sharyl Heiken
Associate Department Heads: Sandra Granseth,
    Rosemary C. Hutchinson, Elizabeth Woolever
Senior Food Editors: Linda Henry, Mary Jo Plutt,
    Joyce Trollope
Associate Food Editors: Jennifer Darling, Debra-Ann Duggan,
    Heather M. Hephner, Mary Major, Shelli McConnell
Test Kitchen: Director, Sharon Stilwell; Photo Studio Director,
    Janet Herwig; Home Economists: Lynn Blanchard, Kay Cargill,
    Marilyn Cornelius, Maryellyn Krantz, Marge Steenson,
    Colleen Weeden

Associate Art Directors: Neoma Thomas, Linda Ford Vermie,
    Randall Yontz
Assistant Art Directors: Lynda Haupert, Harijs Priekulis,
    Tom Wegner
Graphic Designers: Mary Schlueter Bendgen, Michael Burns,
    Brenda Lesch
Art Production: Director, John Berg; Associate, Joe Heuer;
    Office Manager, Michaela Lester

President, Book Group: Jeramy Lanigan
Vice President, Retail Marketing: Jamie Martin
Vice President, Administrative Services: Rick Rundall

BETTER HOMES AND GARDENS® MAGAZINE
President, Magazine Group: James A. Autry
Vice President, Editorial Director: Doris Eby
Food and Nutrition Editor: Nancy Byal

MEREDITH CORPORATE OFFICERS
Chairman of the Executive Committee: E. T. Meredith III
Chairman of the Board: Robert A. Burnett
President: Jack D. Rehm

SUMMERTIME COOKING

Editor: Heather M. Hephner
Project Manager: Liz Anderson
Graphic Designer: Tom Wegner
Electronic Text Processor: Paula Forest
Food Stylists: Lynn Blanchard, Janet Herwig
Contributing Photographers: Michael Dieter, Sean Fitzgerald,
    Scott Little
Contributing Illustrator: Buck Jones

On the cover: *Apple-Chicken Salad* (see recipe, page 44)

Contents

4 Taking It Easy

An introduction to warm-weather cooking.
Too-Hot-to-Cook Menu: A no-cook meal to help beat the heat.

8 No-Sweat Main Dishes

Easy-on-the-cook recipes for the skillet, wok, broiler, or crockery cooker.

24 Bumper Crop Vegetables

Tasty ideas for using garden-fresh summer vegetables.

26 Fire Up the Grill

Timings for grilled meats, poultry, and fish, plus side-dish grill mates.

32 Cool-Off Sandwiches

A savory assortment of sandwiches.

40 Cool-as-a-Cucumber Salads

Satisfying salads to make mealtime a breeze.

48 Food for a Crowd

A party-pack of ideas for the perfect warm-weather gathering.
Hold-the-Ants! Picnic Menu: A portable summer feast for 6 or 12.

64 Wet Your Whistle

Chilly refreshers to quench summertime thirst.

68 Sweet Conclusions

Palate-pleasin' desserts to scoop up for summer.

76 Bumper Crop Fruit

Fast-fixin' desserts that make the most of fresh fruit.

79 Index

Taking It Easy

It's summer—time to sit back, relax, and enjoy life. With the warm-weather food ideas you'll find here, you can make summer meals a breeze. They're light, fresh, and delicious. And many of the recipes use seasonal fruits, vegetables, and herbs—some of the joys of summer.

What's more, the recipes were streamlined and the cooking techniques were chosen to keep you and your kitchen cool. With a little planning, you can have cool, refreshing, home-cooked meals in minutes.

And when it's too hot to cook, take our advice—don't! Try our Too-Hot-to-Cook Menu on the next three pages. It's a complete meal that requires absolutely no cooking. What could be better in the hot days of summer?

Antipasto Salad
  (see recipe, page 6)
Dilly Beef Sandwiches
  (see recipe, page 7)
No-Bake Fruit Pie
  (see recipe, page 7)
Fruity Summer Punch
  or Iced Tea
  (see recipe, page 67)

Too-Hot-to-Cook Menu

Menu

Antipasto Salad
Dilly Beef Sandwiches
Hard rolls
No-Bake Fruit Pie
Fruity Summer Punch
(See recipe, page 67.)
or
Iced Tea

Menu Countdown

Up to 1 Day Ahead:
Prepare Antipasto Salad;
cover and chill for at
least 2 hours.
More Than 1¼ Hours Ahead:
Prepare No-Bake Fruit
Pie; chill at least 1
hour.
20 Minutes Ahead:
Prepare Fruity Summer
Punch or iced tea. Slice
orange for Fruity
Summer Punch *or* lemon
for iced tea.

10 Minutes Ahead:
Assemble Dilly Beef
Sandwiches.
Just Before Serving:
Arrange salads on lettuce-lined
salad plates and place
sandwiches on other plates.
Put an orange *or* lemon slice
in each glass, and fill with
punch *or* iced tea.
Place rolls in a bread basket or
serving bowl.
Cut fruit pie into serving-size
pieces.

Antipasto Salad

Pictured on page 5.

1 cup cauliflower *or* broccoli
  flowerets
¾ cup sliced zucchini *or*
  yellow squash
3 ounces hard salami *or*
  summer sausage, cut
  into ½-inch cubes
3 ounces mozzarella *or* Swiss
  cheese, cut into ½-inch
  cubes
½ cup halved fresh
  mushrooms
½ medium sweet red *or* green
  pepper, cut into 1-inch
  squares
¼ cup pitted ripe olives
¼ cup Italian salad dressing

● In a large bowl combine cauliflower or
broccoli, zucchini or yellow squash, hard
salami or summer sausage, cheese,
mushrooms, pepper, and olives. Pour
dressing on top; toss to coat. Cover and
chill 2 to 24 hours, stirring occasionally.

**Let your garden be your
guide when creating this
Italian-style salad. As the
summer wears on, switch
the vegetables to use
those that are most
plentiful.**

  Lettuce leaves (optional)
5 to 6 cherry tomatoes *or* 1
  small tomato, cut into
  wedges (optional)

● If desired, serve salad on lettuce-lined
plates and garnish with tomatoes. Makes
4 to 6 side-dish servings.

Nutrition information per serving: 213 calories,
10 g protein, 7 g carbohydrate, 17 g fat, 24 mg
cholesterol, 552 mg sodium, 321 mg potassium.

Dilly Beef Sandwiches

Pictured on pages 4 and 5.

½ of an 8-ounce container
   soft-style cream cheese
   (about ½ cup)
¼ cup dairy sour cream
⅓ cup chopped dill pickle
2 teaspoons snipped fresh
   dillweed *or* ½ teaspoon
   dried dillweed

● For spread, in a small bowl combine cream cheese and sour cream. Stir in pickle and dillweed.

If you like dill, this double-dill combo is right up your alley! It's great in the winter, too. Just add a bowl of soup and you've got a whole meal.

8 slices rye bread
12 ounces thinly sliced roast
   beef, corned beef, *or*
   pastrami
4 lettuce leaves
1 large tomato, sliced

● Spread *one side* of *each* bread slice generously with the cream cheese spread. Then place a few slices of meat, a lettuce leaf, and tomato slice on each of *one-half* of the bread slices; top with remaining bread slices, spread-side down. Makes 4 servings.

Nutrition information per serving: 415 calories, 32 g protein, 30 g carbohydrate, 19 g fat, 66 mg cholesterol, 614 mg sodium, 569 mg potassium

No-Bake Fruit Pie

Pictured on page 4.

1 8-ounce package cream
   cheese, softened
¼ cup sugar
2 teaspoons shredded
   orange peel
2 tablespoons orange juice
   or orange liqueur

● In a mixing bowl combine cream cheese, sugar, orange peel, and orange juice or orange liqueur till smooth.

This speedy no-bake pie uses a purchased pie shell and takes advantage of great-tasting fresh fruit. What could be simpler?

1 butter-flavored *or* graham-
   cracker-crumb pie shell
4 cups sliced fresh peaches
1 tablespoon lemon juice
1 cup fresh blueberries

● Carefully spread cream cheese mixture into pie shell. Toss peaches with lemon juice to prevent browning. Arrange the peaches and blueberries over the cream cheese mixture.

Sifted powdered sugar
   (optional)

● Chill for 1 to 24 hours. If desired, sprinkle with powdered sugar. Makes 6 to 8 servings.

Nutrition information per serving: 336 calories, 4 g protein, 40 g carbohydrate, 19 g fat, 31 mg cholesterol, 282 mg sodium, 287 mg potassium.

Chicken Marsala with Mushrooms

4 medium skinless, boneless chicken breast halves (12 ounces total)	● Rinse chicken; pat dry with paper towels.	When company is coming and time is short, here's a dish that goes together pronto. Team it up with rice pilaf and a vegetable for a simple, yet elegant meal.
2 cups fresh mushrooms, halved 2 green onions, sliced 1 clove garlic, minced 1 to 2 tablespoons margarine *or* butter	● In a 10-inch skillet cook mushrooms, green onion, and garlic in *1 tablespoon* margarine or butter over medium-high heat till tender, but not brown. Remove from skillet. If necessary, add another tablespoon of margarine. Add chicken to skillet and cook 10 to 12 minutes or till tender and no pink remains, turning once. Remove from skillet; cover to keep warm.	
⅓ cup chicken broth ⅓ cup dry Marsala wine	● Carefully add chicken broth and Marsala wine to skillet. Cook, uncovered, 3 to 4 minutes or till liquid is reduced to ¼ cup. Return chicken and vegetables to skillet. Cover and cook about 1 minute to heat through.	
Hot cooked rice (optional) 2 tablespoons snipped parsley (optional)	● Transfer chicken to a serving platter, then spoon vegetables and broth mixture over chicken. If desired, serve over hot cooked rice and sprinkle with parsley. Makes 4 servings.	

Nutrition information per serving: 197 calories, 28 g protein, 3 g carbohydrate, 6 g fat, 72 mg cholesterol, 164 mg sodium, 406 mg potassium.

Linguine with Zucchini and Kielbasa

6 ounces linguine
¼ cup red wine vinegar
1 tablespoon sugar
1 tablespoon Dijon-style
   mustard
1 teaspoon dried basil,
   crushed

● Cook linguine in boiling salted water according to package directions. Drain. Set aside.
   For dressing, in a small mixing bowl combine vinegar, sugar, Dijon-style mustard, basil, and 2 tablespoons *water*. Set aside.

Zucchini for recipes such as this one is best if used when it is small (about 1 inch in diameter). Save your garden giants to stuff with fillings, such as sausage, bread stuffing, or mixed vegetables.

12 ounces kielbasa, halved
   lengthwise and cut into
   ¼-inch-thick slices
1 medium sweet red *or* green
   pepper, cut into bite-
   size strips
1 medium onion, chopped
2 small zucchini, thinly
   sliced

● In a medium skillet, cook kielbasa, pepper, and onion till kielbasa is heated through and onion is tender. Add dressing and zucchini and cook 2 minutes more. Toss with linguine. Makes 4 servings.

Nutrition information per serving; 461 calories, 18 g protein, 43 g carbohydrate, 24 g fat, 57 mg cholesterol, 1,029 mg sodium, 560 mg potassium.

Saucy Kielbasa: Prepare as above, *except* omit dressing and use 1 cup *spaghetti sauce.*

Nutrition information per serving; 507 calories, 19 g protein, 48 g carbohydrate, 27 g fat, 57 mg cholesterol, 1,216 mg sodium, 759 mg potassium.

Quick-Fix Main Dishes

When you want to cook a meal in a hurry, get into the fast lane with these quick main dishes.

● **Fajitas in a Flash:** Cook frozen beef sandwich steaks according to package directions. Serve in flour tortillas with shredded lettuce, sliced green onion, chopped tomato, and clear Italian salad dressing.
● **Easy Chicken or Fish Parmesan:** Heat frozen chicken or fish fillets according to package directions. Top with spaghetti sauce and shredded Parmesan or mozzarella cheese; heat till cheese melts.
● **Tortilla Roll-Ups:** Fill flour tortillas with deli tuna or chicken salad, lettuce, and tomatoes.

● **Quick Chow Mein:** Prepare canned chicken or beef stew according to package directions. Serve over chow mein noodles.
● **Timesaving Tuna Macaroni Salad:** Add drained tuna and chopped radishes to deli macaroni salad. Serve on a bed of lettuce.
● **Snappy Peas and Ham:** Cook a package of frozen cream-sauced peas or other creamed vegetable according to package directions. Add chunks of fully cooked ham. Serve over biscuits or corn bread and top with shredded cheddar cheese.

Seafood Skillet Stir-Fry

12 ounces fresh *or* frozen
    shrimp in shells *or* 10
    ounces frozen, peeled
    and deveined shrimp
8 ounces fresh *or* frozen
    scallops
½ cup dry white wine
4 teaspoons cornstarch
1 tablespoon white wine
    Worcestershire sauce
2 teaspoons instant chicken
    bouillon granules

● Thaw shrimp and scallops, if frozen. If necessary, shell and devein shrimp. Set aside.

In a bowl combine, wine, cornstarch, Worcestershire sauce, bouillon granules, ½ cup *water,* and ⅛ teaspoon *pepper.* Set aside.

Rice is nice, but for a change, serve this skillet dish over hot cooked orzo or warmed chow mein noodles.

---

2 cups sliced fresh
    mushrooms
1 medium sweet red *or* green
    pepper, cut into ½-inch
    pieces
½ cup sliced celery
⅓ cup sliced green onion
1 clove garlic, minced
2 tablespoons olive *or*
    cooking oil

● In a wok stir-fry mushrooms, red pepper, celery, onion, and garlic in *1 tablespoon* of the oil over medium-high heat for 3 to 4 minutes till crisp-tender (see tip, page 16). Remove vegetable mixture.

Add remaining oil to wok. Add scallops. Stir-fry 2 to 3 minutes or till scallops are opaque. Remove; set aside. Add shrimp to wok, stir-fry 2 to 3 minutes or till pink. Remove; set aside.

---

2 tablespoons snipped
    parsley
  Hot cooked rice (optional)
  Lemon wedges (optional)

● Stir cornstarch mixture; add to wok. Cook and stir till thickened and bubbly; return vegetables and seafood to wok. Cook about 1 minute or till heated through. Sprinkle with parsley. If desired, serve over rice with lemon. Serves 4.

● **Microwave Directions:** Thaw shrimp and scallops, if frozen. If necessary, shell and devein shrimp.

For cornstarch mixture, in a 2-cup glass measure combine wine, cornstarch, Worcestershire sauce, bouillon granules, ⅓ cup *water,* and ⅛ teaspoon *pepper.* Cook, uncovered, on 100% power (high) 1½ to 2½ minutes or till thickened and bubbly; stir after *every* minute. Set aside.

In a 2-quart casserole, combine mushrooms, red pepper, celery, onion, garlic, and oil. Cook, covered, on high 3 minutes. Add shrimp and scallops. Cook, covered, for 3 to 4 minutes or till scallops are opaque, stirring twice. Drain. Stir cornstarch mixture. Stir into seafood mixture. Cook, uncovered, 1 to 2 minutes or till hot. Serve as above.

Nutrition information per serving: 248 calories, 25 g protein, 11 g carbohydrate, 9 g fat, 126 mg cholesterol, 441 mg sodium, 612 mg potassium.

Fish Steaks with Zucchini Mayonnaise

2 fresh *or* frozen swordfish, salmon, halibut, *or* shark steaks, cut 1 to 1¼ inches thick (about 1½ pounds) **1 cup dry white wine** **¾ cup water** **½ teaspoon dried tarragon, crushed**	● Cut fish steaks into four equal portions. In a large skillet combine wine, water, and tarragon. Bring just to boiling. Carefully add fish. Return to boiling; reduce heat. Cover and simmer till fish just flakes with a fork. Allow 8 to 12 minutes for 1-inch-thick fish steaks and 10 to 15 minutes for 1¼-inch-thick fish steaks (see photos, right). Remove the fish steaks from the water and drain thoroughly on paper towels.
½ of a small zucchini, very thinly sliced (about ½ cup) **¼ cup mayonnaise *or* salad dressing** **¼ cup plain yogurt** **⅛ teaspoon dried tarragon, crushed**	● Meanwhile, for sauce, in a small bowl stir together the zucchini, mayonnaise or salad dressing, yogurt, and tarragon.

● To serve, spoon some of the sauce over each fish portion. Makes 4 servings.

Nutrition information per serving: 338 calories, 30 g protein, 4 g carbohydrate, 17 g fat, 66 mg cholesterol, 224 mg sodium, 550 mg potassium.

Undercooked fish looks translucent, and has clear, watery juices. When tested with a fork, the flesh is very firm and doesn't flake easily.

Properly cooked fish has milky white juices and looks opaque. When tested with a fork, the flesh flakes easily, separating readily from any bones.

Overcooked fish is opaque and there are few juices visible. When tested with a fork, the flesh breaks into small pieces and is very dry.

Orange-Sauced Pork Chops

4 pork rib chops (1¼ pounds total) 1 tablespoon cooking oil ¼ teaspoon salt ⅛ teaspoon pepper	● In a large skillet cook pork chops in hot oil on both sides till brown. Drain off any fat from the skillet and discard. Sprinkle chops with salt and pepper.	**Our taste testers thought these tender orange-flavored pork chops were perfect with couscous, a North African pastalike side dish. You'll find couscous in the rice section at the grocery store.**
3 large oranges	● Finely shred *2 teaspoons* orange peel. Squeeze *1 cup* orange juice. Set aside peel and ½ *cup* of the juice. Add the remaining ½ *cup* orange juice to skillet and cook chops, covered, over low heat for 30 minutes till meat is tender. Remove the pork chops from skillet; keep warm. Do not drain skillet.	
1 tablespoon all-purpose flour 1 teaspoon sugar	● For sauce, in a small bowl combine the flour and sugar. Stir in the set-aside orange peel and orange juice. Add the mixture to the juices in the skillet. Cook and stir over medium heat till sauce is thickened and bubbly. Cook and stir 1 minute more.	
2 cups hot cooked couscous	● Serve sauce with pork chops and couscous. Makes 4 servings.	

Nutrition information per serving: 347 calories, 24 g protein, 33 g carbohydrate, 13 g fat, 54 mg cholesterol, 158 mg sodium, 412 mg potassium.

Beef and Fresh Tomato Stir-Fry

1 **pound flank steak**	● Partially freeze beef; bias-slice across the grain into thin bite-size strips (*see* tip, page 16). In a mixing bowl combine soy sauce, cooking oil, and cornstarch. Add beef to soy sauce mixture; toss strips to coat. Cover and marinate for 2 to 8 hours in the refrigerator.
2 **tablespoons soy sauce**	
2 **tablespoons cooking oil**	
1 **teaspoon cornstarch**	

1 **cup tomato juice**	● In a small bowl combine tomato juice, cornstarch, sugar, soy sauce, and Worcestershire sauce. Set aside.
1 **tablespoon cornstarch**	
1 **tablespoon sugar**	
1 **tablespoon soy sauce**	
2 **teaspoons Worcestershire sauce**	

1 **tablespoon cooking oil**	● Preheat wok or large skillet over high heat; add cooking oil. (Add more oil during cooking as necessary.) Add gingerroot and stir-fry 15 seconds. Add green onions and pepper. Stir-fry for 2 minutes. Remove vegetables from the wok or skillet.
1 **teaspoon grated gingerroot**	
2 **green onions, sliced**	
1 **medium green *or* sweet yellow pepper, cut into bite-size strips**	

| 1 **tablespoon cooking oil** | ● Add oil and *half* of the *undrained* flank steak and stir-fry 2 to 3 minutes or till meat is brown. Remove from wok or skillet. Stir-fry remaining meat. |

| 2 **medium tomatoes, cut into thin wedges**
 Hot cooked rice (optional) | ● Return all the meat to the wok or skillet. Push meat from center of wok. Stir tomato juice mixture and pour in center; cook and stir till thickened and bubbly. Return stir-fried vegetables to wok. Add tomatoes. Stir all ingredients together to coat with sauce. Cover and cook 1 to 2 minutes more to heat through. If desired, serve over hot cooked rice. Makes 4 servings. |

Nutrition information per serving: 339 calories, 19 g protein, 14 g carbohydrate, 24 g fat, 46 mg cholesterol, 1,078 mg sodium, 619 mg potassium.

Stir-Fried Pork in Hoisin Sauce

1 **pound lean boneless pork**
¼ **cup soy sauce**
2 **tablespoons sherry**
2 **tablespoons hoisin sauce**
1 **tablespoon cornstarch**
1 **tablespoon sugar**
1 **to 1½ teaspoons crushed red pepper**

1 **tablespoon cooking oil**
2 **cloves garlic minced**
1 **teaspoon grated gingerroot**
1 **medium zucchini _or_ yellow squash, halved lengthwise _and_ sliced into ¼-inch slices**
1 **cup mushrooms, halved**
4 **green onions, sliced**
1 **8-ounce can sliced water chestnuts, drained**

● Partially freeze pork; bias-slice across the grain into thin bite-size strips. Set aside (see photo, right).

In a small bowl combine soy sauce, sherry, hoisin sauce, cornstarch, sugar, crushed red pepper, and ⅓ cup _water_. Set aside.

● Preheat wok or large skillet over medium-high heat; add cooking oil. (Add more oil as necessary during cooking.) Stir-fry garlic and gingerroot in hot oil for 15 seconds. Add zucchini or squash and mushrooms and stir-fry for 2 minutes. Add onions and water chestnuts. Stir-fry 1 minute more. Remove vegetable mixture.

Add _half_ of the pork. Stir-fry 2 to 3 minutes or till no pink remains. Remove pork. Add remaining pork and stir-fry 2 to 3 minutes. Return all pork to wok or skillet. Push from center of wok.

Stir soy mixture; add to center of wok or skillet. Cook and stir till thickened and bubbly. Return vegetables to wok or skillet. Cook and stir for 1 minute. Makes 4 or 5 servings.

Nutrition information per serving: 268 calories, 21 g protein, 16 g carbohydrate, 13 g fat, 61 mg cholesterol, 933 mg sodium, 644 mg potassium.

This recipe is so quick, it's a real flash in the pan. If you don't have a wok, use a skillet with high sides.

To bias-slice meat, first partially freeze it (about 40 to 45 minutes for a 1-inch-thick piece). Hold a knife at a slight angle to the cutting surface. Slice across the grain of the meat, making very thin slices (about ⅛ inch thick) that are 2 to 3 inches long.

Stir-Frying Tips

Summertime is stir-frying time. Why? Because with this _easy_ technique, fresh vegetables retain their crispness and color, and meats come out tender and flavorful. An added bonus for the hot-weather cook is that stir-frying is fast so the kitchen stays cool.

● A wok is easiest for stir-frying because its shape offers a large surface and even distribution of heat. But large, deep skillets work great, too.
● It's important to have everything ready before you start stir-frying. Slice the meat, mix the sauce, and cut the vegetables before you turn on the heat.
● Stir-fry on the highest setting of your range, but lower the heat, if necessary, to prevent scorching.
● Using a spatula or long-handled spoon, gently lift and turn the pieces of food with a folding motion. Keep the food moving for even cooking.

Cashew Chicken Stir-Fry

2 cups fresh pea pods *or* one 6-ounce package frozen pea pods ⅔ cup cold water 2 tablespoons soy sauce 2 teaspoons cornstarch ½ teaspoon instant chicken bouillon granules	● Run warm water over pea pods, if frozen. Drain well. Halve; set aside. In a small bowl combine water, soy sauce, cornstarch, and bouillon granules. Set aside.
1 tablespoon cooking oil 2 cloves garlic, minced 1 to 2 teaspoons grated gingerroot 2 carrots, bias-sliced ⅛ inch thick 3 green onions, sliced	● Preheat wok or large skillet over high heat; add cooking oil. (Add more oil as necessary during cooking.) Add garlic, and gingerroot. Stir-fry 30 seconds (see tip, page 16). Add carrots; stir-fry 2 minutes. Add green onions; stir-fry 1 minute more or until carrots are crisp-tender. Remove vegetable mixture.
1 tablespoon cooking oil 3 skinless, boneless chicken breast halves, cut into bite-size strips (about 9 ounces)	● Add cooking oil to the hot wok or skillet. Add chicken; stir-fry 2 to 3 minutes or till chicken is tender and no pink remains. Push chicken from center of wok.
½ cup cashews Hot cooked rice (optional)	● Stir cornstarch mixture, then add to the center of the wok or skillet. Cook and stir till thickened and bubbly. Return vegetables to wok or skillet. Stir in pea pods. Cook 2 minutes more or till heated through. Stir in cashews. If desired, serve over hot cooked rice. Makes 4 servings.

If you love crunch, you'll be nutty about this dish. Nuts and crisp vegetables make it burst with both flavor and crunch.

Nutrition information per serving: 320 calories, 25 g protein, 17 g carbohydrate, 17 g fat, 54 mg cholesterol, 623 mg sodium, 555 mg potassium.

Walnut Chicken: Prepare Cashew Chicken Stir-Fry as above, *except* substitute walnut pieces for the cashews.

Nutrition information per serving: 300 calories, 25 g protein, 13 g carbohydrate, 17 g fat, 54 mg cholesterol, 621 mg sodium, 519 mg potassium.

Almond Chicken: Prepare Cashew Chicken Stir-Fry as above, *except* substitute whole blanched almonds for the cashews.

Nutrition information per serving: 317 calories, 26 g protein, 14 g carbohydrate, 18 g fat, 54 mg cholesterol, 622 mg sodium, 577 mg potassium.

Crab-Stuffed Lobster Tails

4 5-ounce frozen lobster tails, thawed	● Use kitchen shears to cut a lengthwise slit through back and meat of *each* lobster tail (*see* photo, right). Using fingers, press tail open, exposing meat. Set lobster tails aside.

2 tablespoons sliced green
    onion
1 tablespoon sliced celery
1 tablespoon margarine *or*
    butter
1½ teaspoons all-purpose
    flour
⅛ teaspoon dry mustard
    Dash ground red pepper
⅓ cup milk *or* light cream
½ of a 6-ounce package
    frozen crabmeat,
    thawed
2 tablespoons plain
    croutons, coarsely
    crushed

● For stuffing, in a small saucepan cook green onion and celery in margarine or butter till tender but not brown. Stir in flour, mustard, and red pepper. Add milk or cream. Cook and stir till thickened and bubbly. Cook and stir 1 minute more. Remove from heat. Gently stir in crabmeat and croutons.

Slitting the lobster tails helps them lie flat and cook evenly. This technique is often called butterflying. Here's how you go about it. First, cut through the center of the hard top shell of the lobster tails with kitchen shears or a sharp, heavy knife. Do not cut through the bottom shell. Then, spread the meat open in the shell.

● Preheat broiler. Place lobster tails, split-side up, on rack of unheated broiler pan. Broil 4 inches from the heat for 6 to 7 minutes or till lobster meat is just opaque. Top with stuffing and broil 2 to 3 minutes more till heated through. Makes 4 servings.

● **Grilling Directions:** Top split lobster tails with stuffing. Grill in a covered grill directly over *medium-hot* coals about 12 minutes or till lobster meat is opaque. Makes 4 servings.

Nutrition information per serving: 136 calories, 20 g protein, 4 g carbohydrate, 4 g fat, 64 mg cholesterol, 552 mg sodium, 352 mg potassium.

Broiled Beef

¾ to 1 pound beef flank steak
½ cup steak sauce
¼ cup dry red wine
2 tablespoons water
1 clove garlic, minced
½ teaspoon dried thyme, crushed
¼ teaspoon pepper

● Preheat broiler. Score meat by making shallow cuts at 1-inch intervals diagonally across steak in a diamond pattern. Repeat on second side.

For sauce, in a small bowl stir together steak sauce, wine, water, garlic, thyme, and pepper. Place steak on unheated rack of a broiler pan. Brush with sauce. Broil 3 inches from the heat for 12 to 14 minutes for medium, turning once and brushing with a little more sauce.

2 cups sliced mushrooms
1 tablespoon margarine *or* butter

● Meanwhile, in a medium skillet, cook and stir mushrooms in margarine or butter over medium-high heat for 4 to 5 minutes or till tender. Just before serving, stir in remaining sauce.

Thinly slice steak diagonally across the grain. Serve mushrooms over sliced steak. Makes 4 servings.

Nutrition information per serving: 238 calories, 18 g protein, 9 g carbohydrate, 13 g fat, 45 mg cholesterol, 737 mg sodium, 600 mg potassium.

This tangy, saucy beef dish also tastes great cooked on the grill. Prepare as the recipe indicates, *except* place the steak on the rack of an uncovered grill over *medium* coals for 12 to 14 minutes, turning once.

Fish with Tarragon

4 fresh *or* frozen orange roughy *or* whitefish fillets (about 1 pound)

● Thaw fish, if frozen. Rinse and pat dry with paper towels.

¼ cup chopped green onions
2 tablespoons margarine *or* butter, melted
1 tablespoon finely snipped fresh tarragon *or* 2 teaspoons dried tarragon, crushed
¼ teaspoon finely shredded lemon peel
¼ teaspoon pepper

● Preheat broiler. For sauce, in a small mixing bowl combine the onions, melted margarine or butter, tarragon, lemon peel, and pepper.

Measure thickness of fillets. Place fillets on the rack of an unheated broiler pan. Brush with the sauce. Broil 4 inches from the heat for 4 to 6 minutes per ½-inch thickness or till fish flakes easily with a fork. Makes 4 servings.

Grilling Directions: Place fillets in a greased wire grill basket. Place basket on an uncovered grill directly over *medium-hot* coals. Grill about 4 to 6 minutes per ½-inch thickness or till done.

Nutrition information per serving: 198 calories, 17 g protein, 1 g carbohydrate, 14 g fat, 23 mg cholesterol, 139 mg sodium, 416 mg potassium.

Fresh herbs, such as the tarragon in this recipe, are one of the joys of summer. If you don't have any tarragon, try basil, rosemary, dill, or another herb of your choice.

Swordfish Kabobs

1 **pound fresh *or* frozen swordfish steaks**	● Thaw fish, if frozen. Cut into 1-inch pieces. Place in plastic bag; set in bowl.
2 **tablespoons snipped parsley** 2 **tablespoons snipped fresh basil *or* 2 teaspoons dried basil, crushed** 2 **tablespoons white wine vinegar** 2 **tablespoons white wine Worcestershire sauce** 1 **tablespoon cooking oil** ¼ **teaspoon garlic salt** ⅛ **teaspoon pepper**	● For marinade, in a small mixing bowl combine parsley, basil, vinegar, Worcestershire sauce, cooking oil, garlic salt, and pepper. Pour over fish in bag. Close bag and marinate at room temperature for 20 minutes, turning bag occasionally to distribute marinade.
10 **to 12 green onions, cut into 3-inch pieces** 2 **medium sweet red peppers, cut into 1-inch pieces**	● Drain fish, reserving marinade. Using four 15-inch skewers, alternately thread green onions, red pepper, and fish, leaving about ¼ inch of space between pieces.
	● Place kabobs on greased rack of an unheated broiler pan. Broil 4 to 6 inches from the heat for 4 to 6 minutes or till fish flakes easily with a fork. Turn and brush fish often with the reserved marinade. Makes 4 servings.

● **Grilling Directions:** Lightly grease a cold grill rack. Place kabobs on rack. Position rack directly over *medium* coals on an uncovered grill. Grill for 8 to 12 minutes or till fish flakes easily with a fork. Turn and brush fish often with the reserved marinade.

Nutrition information per serving: 160 calories, 20 g protein, 5 g carbohydrate, 6 g fat, 38 mg cholesterol, 222 mg sodium, 464 mg potassium.

The trick to getting kabobs evenly done is to leave a little space between pieces as you thread the chunks on a skewer.

Mariner's Garden Chowder

1   14½-ounce can chicken broth
1   12-ounce can vegetable juice cocktail
2   medium tomatoes, chopped
1   medium carrot, thinly sliced
1   stalk celery, sliced
1   tablespoon snipped fresh basil *or* 1 teaspoon dried basil, crushed
1   tablespoon snipped fresh thyme *or* 1 teaspoon dried thyme, crushed
⅛   teaspoon salt
⅛   teaspoon pepper

● In a 3½- or 4-quart crockery cooker, combine chicken broth, vegetable juice cocktail, tomatoes, carrot, celery, basil, thyme, salt, and pepper. Cover; cook on low-heat setting for 9½ to 11½ hours or on high-heat setting for 4 to 5 hours or till vegetables are tender.

On hot summer days, there's no need to spend a lot of time preparing meals. Just bring out your crockery cooker and let the meal cook unattended. Serve this flavorful soup with a crusty roll for a light meal. Or, for a more hearty meal, try the Crockery Barbecued Beef on the next page.

3   6½-ounce cans minced clams
½   cup quick-cooking rice
1   tablespoon snipped parsley *or* 1 teaspoon dried parsley, crushed
¼   cup grated Parmesan cheese

● Stir in *undrained* clams and rice. (If using low setting, turn crockery cooker to high.) Cover and cook for 10 minutes more. Stir in parsley. Ladle into bowls. Serve with grated Parmesan cheese. Makes 4 servings.

Nutrition information per serving: 313 calories, 40 g protein, 26 g carbohydrate, 4 g fat, 94 mg cholesterol, 937 mg sodium, 1,341 mg potassium.

Keep the Lid On It!

Although you may be tempted, resist the urge to remove the lid to peek into your crockery cooker, especially when cooking on the low-heat setting. If you leave the cooker uncovered, it can lose as much as 20 degrees of important cooking heat in only two minutes. So, if you must peek, make it *quick* and replace the lid immediately.

Crockery Barbecued Beef

¾ cup cola (*not* diet)
¼ cup Worcestershire sauce
1 tablespoon vinegar
2 cloves garlic, minced
1 teaspoon instant beef bouillon granules
½ teaspoon dry mustard
½ teaspoon chili powder
¼ teaspoon ground red pepper
1 1½-pound boneless beef chuck roast

● For cooking liquid, in a bowl combine cola, Worcestershire sauce, vinegar, garlic, bouillon granules, mustard, chili powder, and red pepper; reserve ½ cup cooking liquid for sauce.

Trim excess fat from meat. Cut meat to fit into a 3½- to 4-quart crockery cooker.

What's the secret ingredient hiding in this crockery-cooker beef? Cola! Besides a distinctive flavor, it gives the barbecue sauce its sweetness and its rich color.

2 medium onions, chopped

● Place onions and meat in the crockery cooker. Pour remaining cooking liquid over meat. Cover and cook 10 to 12 hours on low-heat setting or 5 to 6 hours on high heat setting.

½ cup catsup
2 tablespoons margarine *or* butter
Shredded greens *or* flour tortillas (optional)

● Meanwhile, for sauce, in a small saucepan combine the ½ cup reserved cooking liquid, catsup, and margarine. Heat through. Set sauce aside.

Transfer meat to a cutting board and shred. Discard cooking liquid.

If desired, serve meat on a bed of shredded greens or with greens in flour tortillas. Pass sauce. Makes 6 servings.

Nutrition information per serving: 290 calories, 29 g protein, 13 g carbohydrate, 13 g fat, 86 mg cholesterol, 508 mg sodium, 389 mg potassium.

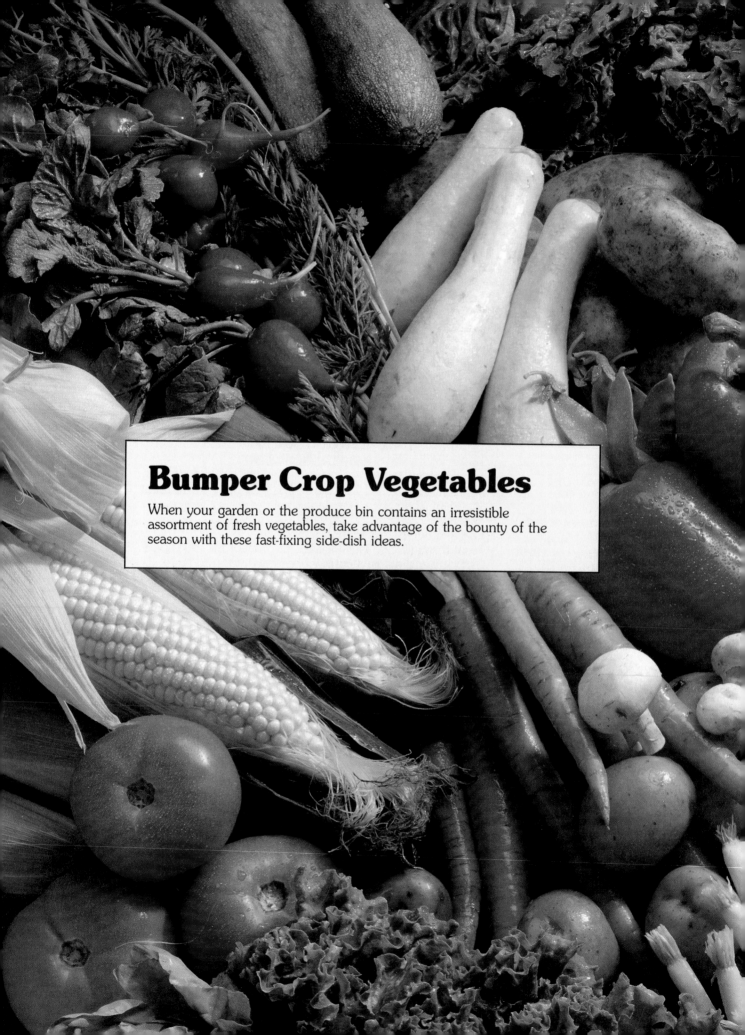

Bumper Crop Vegetables

When your garden or the produce bin contains an irresistible assortment of fresh vegetables, take advantage of the bounty of the season with these fast-fixing side-dish ideas.

Lemon-Herb Buttered Vegetables:

Cook vegetables as directed in Cheese-Sauced Vegetables, *except* for sauce, in saucepan combine 1 tablespoon *snipped parsley;* 1 tablespoon *margarine or butter;* 2 teaspoons *lemon juice;* ¼ teaspoon *dried marjoram, thyme, basil, savory, or dillweed;* ⅛ teaspoon *salt;* and ⅛ teaspoon *pepper.* Heat till margarine melts. Toss with vegetables. Serves 4.

Nutrition information per serving: 27 calories, 0 g protein, 0 g carbohydrate, 3 g fat, 0 mg cholesterol, 100 mg sodium, 11 mg potassium.

Vegetables with Nuts:

Prepare Lemon-Herb Buttered Vegetables, *except* stir 2 tablespoons coarsely chopped *cashews, pecans, or walnuts* into melted margarine mixture. Makes 4 servings.

Nutrition information per serving: 53 calories, 1 g protein, 2 g carbohydrate, 5 g fat, 0 mg cholesterol, 101 mg sodium, 36 mg potassium.

Cheese-Sauced Vegetables:

In a covered saucepan, cook 3 cups *fresh vegetables* (such as cut asparagus, broccoli or cauliflower flowerets, brussels sprouts, sliced carrots, lima beans, green or yellow beans, or peas) in a small amount of boiling salted water, till crisp-tender. Drain.

For cheese sauce, in a saucepan combine ½ cup *milk or cream* and 2 teaspoons *all-purpose flour.* Cook and stir till slightly thickened. Add ½ cup shredded *American, cheddar or Monterey Jack cheese* and 2 tablespoons snipped *parsley;* cook and stir till cheese melts. Stir in cooked vegetables. Makes 4 servings.

Nutrition information per serving: 103 calories, 6 g protein, 9 g carbohydrate, 5 g fat, 16 mg cholesterol, 235 mg sodium, 369 mg potassium.

Icy Salsa Garden Soup:

In a large mixing bowl combine one 16-ounce jar *mild chunky-style salsa,* one 12-ounce can *tomato juice,* 1 diced medium *carrot,* ½ cup sliced *celery,* and 1 finely minced *garlic clove.* Refrigerate 2 to 24 hours.

Garnish with *ice cubes* and *snipped parsley.* Serves 4 to 6.

Nutrition information per serving: 67 calories, 1 g protein, 14 g carbohydrate, 0 g fat, 0 mg cholesterol, 1,109 mg sodium, 555 potassium.

Grilling Charts

Refer to the charts on these two pages and on page 28 when you want to know the basic grilling times for meats, fish, and poultry. Remember that cuts vary in shape so it's best to check for doneness frequently.

Direct-Grilling Fish

Place fresh fillets* in a well-greased grill basket. Place fresh fish steaks and other seafood on a greased grill rack.

Test for desired temperature of the coals (see tip, page 30). Place fish on the grill directly over the preheated coals. Grill, uncovered, turning once. Brush with melted margarine or butter, if necessary (see Barbecue Brush-Ons, page 29). Cook for the specified time or till the fish flakes when tested with a fork (see photos, page 12). Lobster and sea scallops look opaque, and shrimp turn pink when done. If desired, serve lemon wedges with fish.

*Note: Grilling frozen fillets or steaks is not recommended.

Form of Fish	Size	Coal Temp.	Time
Fresh fillets or steaks	½ to 1 inch thick	medium-hot	4 to 6 minutes per ½-inch thickness
Dressed	½ to 1½ pounds	medium-hot	7 to 9 minutes
Lobster tails	6 to 8 ounces	medium-hot	6 to 10 minutes for 6 ounces; 12 to 15 minutes for 8 ounces
Sea scallops for kabobs	12 to 15 per pound	medium-hot	5 to 8 minutes
Shrimp, peeled and deveined, for kabobs	medium shrimp (about 20 per pound); jumbo (about 12 to 15 per pound)	medium-hot	6 to 8 minutes for medium; 10 to 12 minutes for jumbo

Direct-Grilling Poultry

Remove the skin from the poultry, if desired. Rinse and pat dry with paper towels. If desired, sprinkle with salt and pepper.

Test for desired temperature of the coals (see tip, page 30). Place poultry on the grill, bone side up, directly over the preheated coals. (For ground turkey patties, use a grill basket.) Grill, uncovered, for the specified time or till no pink remains. Turn the poultry over after half of the cooking time. During the last 10 minutes, brush often with sauce, if desired.

Note: When testing for doneness, keep in mind that the white meat will cook slightly faster than the dark.

Type of Bird	Weight	Coal Temp.	Time
Broiler-fryer chicken halves	1¼ to 1½ pounds each	medium	40 to 50 minutes
Chicken breast halves, thighs, and drumsticks	2 to 2½ pounds total	medium	35 to 45 minutes
Chicken breasts, skinned and boned	4 to 5 ounces each	medium-hot	15 to 18 minutes
Chicken kabobs (boneless breasts, cut into 2x½-inch strips and threaded loosely onto skewers)	1 pound total	medium-hot	8 to 10 minutes
Cornish game hen halves	½ to ¾ pound each	medium-hot	45 to 50 minutes
Turkey breast tenderloin steaks	4 to 6 ounces each	medium	12 to 15 minutes
Turkey drumsticks	½ to 1½ pounds each	medium	¾ to 1¼ hours
Turkey hindquarters	2 to 4 pounds each	medium	1¼ to 1½ hours
Turkey patties (ground raw turkey)	¾ inch thick	medium-hot	15 to 18 minutes
Turkey thigh	1 to 1½ pounds	medium	50 to 60 minutes

Indirect-Grilling Meat

In a grill with a cover, arrange *medium* coals around a drip pan (see page 31). Pour 1 inch of water into the drip pan. Test for *medium-low* heat above the pan, unless the chart says otherwise. Insert a meat thermometer into the meat.

Place the meat, fat side up, on the grill rack over the drip pan but not over the coals. Lower the grill hood. Grill for the time given or till the thermometer registers the desired temperature. Add more coals and water as necessary.

Cut	Weight (Pounds)	Doneness	Time (Hours)
Beef			
Boneless rolled rump roast	4 to 6	150° to 170°	1¼ to 2½
Boneless sirloin roast	4 to 6	140° rare	1¾ to 2¼
		160° medium	2¼ to 2¾
		170° well-done	2½ to 3
Eye round roast	2 to 3	140° rare	1 to 1½
		160° medium	1½ to 2
		170° well-done	1¾ to 2¼
Rib eye roast	4 to 6	140° rare	1 to 1½
		160° medium	1½ to 2
		170° well-done	2 to 2½
Rib roast	4 to 6	140° rare	2¼ to 2¾
		160° medium	2¾ to 3¼
		170° well-done	3¼ to 3¾
Tenderloin roast			
Half	2 to 3	140° rare	¾ to 1
Whole	4 to 6	140° rare	1¼ to 1½
(test for *medium-hot* heat above the pan)			
Tip roast	3 to 5	140° to 170°	1¼ to 2½
	6 to 8	140° to 170°	2 to 3¼
Top round roast	4 to 6	140° to 170°	1 to 2
Veal			
Boneless rolled breast roast	2½ to 3½	170° well-done	1¾ to 2¼
Boneless rolled shoulder roast	3 to 5	170° well-done	2¼ to 2¾
Loin roast	3 to 5	170° well-done	2¼ to 2¾
Rib roast	3 to 5	170° well-done	2¼ to 2¾

Cut	Weight (Pounds)	Doneness	Time (Hours)
Lamb			
Boneless leg roast	4 to 7	160° medium	2¼ to 2¾
Boneless rolled shoulder roast	2 to 3	160° medium	1¾ to 2¼
Rib crown roast	3 to 4	140° rare	¾ to 1
		160° medium	¾ to 1
		170° well-done	1 to 1¼
Whole leg roast	5 to 7	140° rare	1¾ to 2¼
		160° medium	2¼ to 2½
		170° well-done	2½ to 3
Pork			
Boneless top loin roast			
Single loin	2 to 4	170° well-done	1 to 2¼
Double loin, tied	3 to 5	170° well-done	1½ to 3
Loin back ribs, spareribs, country-style ribs (test for *medium* heat above the pan)	2 to 4	Well-done	1 to 2
Loin blade or sirloin roast	3 to 4	170° well-done	1¾ to 3
Loin center rib roast (backbone loosened)	3 to 5	170° well-done	1½ to 3
Rib crown roast	4 to 6	170° well-done	1¾ to 3
Tenderloin	¾ to 1	170° well-done	½ to ¾
Ham (fully cooked)			
Boneless half	4 to 6	140°	1¼ to 2½
Boneless portion	3 to 4	140°	1½ to 2¼
Smoked picnic	5 to 8	140°	2 to 3

Direct-Grilling Meat

Test for the desired coal temperature (see tip, page 30). Grill the meat, uncovered, for the time specified in the chart or till done, turning the meat over after half of the cooking time. If desired, season to taste with salt and pepper.

Cut	Thickness (Inches)	Coal Temp.	Doneness	Time (Min.)
Beef				
Flank steak	¾	Medium	Medium	12 to 14
Steak (chuck, blade, top	1	Medium	Rare	14 to 16
			Medium	18 to 20
			Well-done	22 to 24
round)	1½	Medium	Rare	19 to 26
			Medium	27 to 32
			Well-done	33 to 38
Steak (top loin,	1	Medium-hot	Rare	8 to 12
			Medium	12 to 15
tenderloin,			Well-done	16 to 20
T-bone,	1½	Medium-hot	Rare	14 to 18
porterhouse,			Medium	18 to 22
sirloin, rib, rib eye)			Well-done	24 to 28
Veal				
Chop	¾	Medium-hot	Well-done	10 to 12
Lamb				
Chop	1	Medium	Rare	10 to 14
			Medium	14 to 16
			Well-done	16 to 20

Cut	Thickness (Inches)	Coal Temp.	Doneness	Time (Min.)
Pork				
Blade steak	½	Medium-hot	Well-done	10 to 12
Canadian-style bacon	¼	Medium-hot	Heated	3 to 5
Chop	¾	Medium-hot	Well-done	12 to 14
	1¼ to 1½	Medium	Well-done	35 to 45
Ham slice	1	Medium-hot	Heated	20 to 25
Misc.				
Bratwurst, fresh		Medium-hot	Well-done	12 to 14
Cubes (beef, lamb, pork)	1	Medium-hot	Rare	5 to 7
			Medium	6 to 8
			Well-done	8 to 12
Frankfurters		Medium-hot	Heated	3 to 5
Ground-meat patties (beef, lamb, pork)	¾ (4 to a pound)	Medium	Medium	12 to 14
			Well-done	15 to 18

Steak Doneness

How can you tell if steaks are cooked the way your family and guests like them? Use the photos at left as a guide when you test your steaks.

- *Rare* steak is pink on the edges and red in the center.
- *Medium* steak has only a little pink in the center.
- *Well-done* steak is completely cooked with no pink areas at all.

Barbecue Brush-Ons

You can give ordinary grilled foods extra zip by dressing them up with one of these flavored spreads. Since these brush-ons will keep up to two weeks in the refrigerator or one month in the freezer, mix up one or two and keep them on hand. You'll find them delicious and easy to use.

For Meats, Poultry, Fish, and Vegetables:
Flavor ¼ cup softened margarine or butter with one of the following combinations, and spread or brush-on foods before and during cooking:

● **Blue Cheese Butter:** Add ½ teaspoon *lemon juice,* ¼ teaspoon *Worcestershire sauce*, and ⅛ teaspoon *pepper.* Mix thoroughly. Fold in ¼ cup crumbled *blue cheese* and mix just till combined. Serve with meat or baked potatoes. Makes ¼ cup.

Nutrition information per serving: 133 calories, 2 g protein, 0 g carbohydrate, 14 g fat, 6 mg cholesterol, 256 mg sodium, 29 mg potassium.

● **Cajun Butter:** Add ½ teaspoon dried *oregano,* crushed; ¼ teaspoon ground *cumin;* ⅛ teaspoon dried *thyme,* crushed; and dash crushed *red pepper.* Serve with poultry. Makes ¼ cup.

Nutrition information per serving: 104 calories, 0 g protein, 0 g carbohydrate, 12 g fat, 0 mg cholesterol, 135 mg sodium, 13 mg potassium.

● **Fennel Butter:** Add 1 teaspoon *fennel seed,* crushed; ½ teaspoon *lemon juice;* and dash *pepper.* Serve with fish. Makes ¼ cup.

Nutrition information per serving: 104 calories, 0 g protein, 0 g carbohydrate, 12 g fat, 0 mg cholesterol, 135 mg sodium, 16 mg potassium.

● **Lemon-Basil Butter:** Add ½ teaspoon finely shredded *lemon peel,* ½ teaspoon *lemon juice,* and ¼ teaspoon dried *basil,* crushed. Serve with meat, fish, or vegetables. Makes ¼ cup.

Nutrition information per serving: 103 calories, 0 g protein, 0 g carbohydrate, 11 g fat, 0 mg cholesterol, 135 mg sodium, 12 mg potassium.

● **Parmesan Butter:** Add 1 tablespoon grated *Parmesan cheese;* 2 teaspoons snipped *parsley;* and 1 small clove *garlic,* minced. Serve with vegetables. Makes ¼ cup.

Nutrition information per serving: 111 calories, 1 g protein, 0 g carbohydrate, 12 g fat, 1 mg cholesterol, 164 mg sodium, 14 mg potassium.

Breading Spreads:
Slice a 1-pound loaf of white, rye, or wheat French or Italian-style bread into 14 to 16 diagonal slices, cutting to, but not through, bottom crust. Spread your choice of the following spreads between every other slice of bread. Wrap loosely in heavy-duty foil. Place on edge of grill. Grill over *slow* coals about 15 to 20 minutes or till heated through, turning frequently. (Or, wrap loosely in foil and place on a baking sheet. Bake in a 350° oven for 15 to 20 minutes or till heated through.) Makes 14 to 16 single-slice servings.

● **Cheddar-Jalapeño Spread:** Combine 2 tablespoons *softened margarine or butter* and ⅓ cup *cheese spread with jalapeño peppers.* Makes ½ cup.

Nutrition information per serving: 43 calories, 1 g protein, 0 g carbohydrate, 4 g fat, 4 mg cholesterol, 100 mg sodium, 9 mg potassium.

● **Garlic Spread:** Combine ½ cup softened *margarine or butter,* 1 teaspoon *garlic powder,* and ¼ teaspoon *paprika.* Makes ½ cup.

Nutrition information per serving: 103 calories, 0 g protein, 0 g carbohydrate, 11 g fat, 0 mg cholesterol, 134 mg sodium, 11 mg potassium.

● **Italian Herb Spread:** Combine ½ cup softened *margarine or butter;* 1 teaspoon *garlic powder;* ¾ teaspoon *Italian seasoning,* crushed; and 2 tablespoons *grated Parmesan cheese.* Makes ½ cup.

Nutrition information per serving: 111 calories, 1 g protein, 1 g carbohydrate, 12 g fat, 1 mg cholesterol, 163 mg sodium, 14 mg potassium.

● **Tarragon-Onion Spread:** Combine ½ cup softened *margarine* or *butter,* 2 tablespoons *chopped green onion,* 2 tablespoons snipped *parsley,* and ½ teaspoon dried *tarragon,* crushed. Makes ¾ cup.

Nutrition information per serving: 69 calories, 0 g protein, 0 g carbohydrate, 8 g fat, 0 mg cholesterol, 90 mg sodium, 12 mg potassium.

Cheesy Grilled Potatoes

4 slices bacon	● In a skillet cook bacon till crisp. Drain. Crumble bacon; set aside.
4 medium potatoes **¼ cup chopped onion** **¼ teaspoon salt** **⅛ teaspoon pepper** **2 tablespoons margarine *or* butter**	● Tear off a 36x18-inch piece of heavy foil. Fold in half to make an 18-inch square. Fold up sides, forming a pouch. Slice potatoes and place in pouch; add onion. Sprinkle with salt and pepper. Dot with margarine or butter. Fold edges of foil to seal pouch securely, leaving space for steam to expand.
½ cup shredded cheddar cheese *or* Monterey Jack cheese with jalapeño pepper (2 ounces)	● Grill over *medium* coals 35 to 40 minutes or till done, turning over several times. Carefully open pouch. Sprinkle potatoes with crumbled bacon and cheese. Close pouch and let stand 3 to 4 minutes or till cheese is melted. Makes 4 to 6 servings.

Nutrition information per serving: 311 calories, 9 g protein, 39 g carbohydrate, 14 g fat, 20 mg cholesterol, 393 mg sodium, 692 mg potassium.

Keep your kitchen cool. Just toss these potatoes on the grill alongside the main dish.

Zucchini-Tomato Grill

1 medium onion, thinly sliced and separated into rings **2 medium zucchini, thinly sliced** **2 medium tomatoes, sliced**	● On four 18x12-inch pieces of heavy foil layer onion, zucchini, and tomatoes.
2 tablespoons margarine *or* butter **2 tablespoons grated Parmesan cheese** **½ teaspoon Italian seasoning** **Pepper**	● Dot vegetables with margarine or butter. Sprinkle with Parmesan cheese and Italian seasoning. Add pepper to taste. Seal foil packets.
	● Grill over *medium* coals 20 to 25 minutes until vegetables are tender. Makes 4 servings.

Nutrition information per serving: 91 calories, 3 g protein, 6 g carbohydrate, 7 g fat, 2 mg cholesterol, 131 mg sodium, 298 mg potassium.

If you don't have Italian seasoning on hand, substitute ½ teaspoon *each* snipped fresh basil, oregano, and parsley. Or, use ⅛ to ¼ teaspoon *each* of the dried versions.

Chive-Roasted Corn

¼ cup margarine *or* butter, softened
¼ cup fresh snipped chives *or* finely chopped green onion
¼ teaspoon garlic powder
¼ teaspoon pepper
4 ears of corn, husked

● In a small bowl combine margarine or butter, chives or green onion, garlic powder, and pepper. Using a knife, spread ears of corn with butter mixture.

Weather not right for firing up the grill? Then oven-roast the corn at 350° for 30 minutes.

● Wrap each ear in a piece of heavy foil. Grill corn on an uncovered grill directly over *hot* coals for 15 to 18 minutes or till tender, turning frequently. (*Or,* in a covered grill arrange *hot* coals around a drip pan. Place corn on grill rack over drip pan but not over coals. Lower grill hood. Grill 20 to 25 minutes or till tender.) Makes 4 servings.

Nutrition information per serving: 170 calories, 3 g protein, 15 g carbohydrate, 12 g fat, 0 mg cholesterol, 146 mg sodium, 225 mg potassium

How Hot Is It?

For best grilling results, judge the temperature of the coals with this simple test before the food goes on the grill. Hold your hand, palm side down, just above the coals at the height the food will be cooking. The number of seconds you can hold your hand comfortably over the fire tells you the temperature of the coals. Begin counting, "one thousand one," "one thousand two ... " At the count of "one thousand two," coals are *hot* and are perfect for grilling foods that cook quickly, such as steaks, kabobs, and hamburgers. At three seconds, the coals are *medium-hot* and at five or six seconds, the coals are *slow.*

Layered Tortilla Sandwich

2 cups diced cooked chicken (see tip, below) 1 cup shredded lettuce 1 4-ounce can diced green chili peppers, drained 2 tablespoons snipped fresh cilantro *or* parsley	● In a bowl combine chicken, lettuce, chilies, and cilantro or parsley. Set aside.

This tasty tower of tortillas layered with flavorful Mexican ingredients also makes a tempting party appetizer or snack for 16 people.

8 10-inch flour tortillas 1 6-ounce carton frozen avocado dip, thawed 1 16-ounce can refried beans 1 cup dairy sour cream 1½ cups shredded cheddar *or* Monterey Jack cheese (6 ounces)	● Place *one* of the flour tortillas on a large platter. Spread with *half* of the avocado dip. Then top with *a second* tortilla. Spread with *half* of the refried beans. Cover with a *third* tortilla. Sprinkle with *half* of the chicken-lettuce mixture. Add a *fourth* tortilla. Spread with *half* of the sour cream; sprinkle with *half* of the cheese. Repeat layers, ending with sour cream and cheese.

¼ cup chopped tomatoes 2 tablespoons sliced pitted ripe olives 2 tablespoons snipped fresh cilantro *or* parsley Salsa (optional)	● Garnish with tomatoes, olives, and cilantro or parsley. To serve, cut into wedges. If desired, serve with salsa. Makes 8 servings.

Nutrition information per serving: 448 calories, 24 g protein, 43 g carbohydrate, 21 g fat, 67 mg cholesterol, 715 mg sodium, 442 mg potassium

Quick and Easy Cooked Chicken

If your recipe calls for cooked chicken and you don't have any handy, here are two fast and easy ways to get it — poaching or microwaving chicken pieces.

Start with 2 whole medium *chicken breasts* (1½ pounds total), halved lengthwise. (*Or,* use ¾ pound *boneless chicken breasts.*) Either choice yields about 2 cups cut-up cooked chicken.

Poaching Chicken: In a 10-inch skillet bring 1⅓ cups *water* to boiling. Carefully add chicken. Cover and simmer 20 to 25 minutes or till tender. Drain. Cool chicken; remove bones, if necessary, and cut up.

Micro-Cooking Chicken: Place breasts in a 1½-quart microwave-safe casserole. *Do not add liquid.* Micro-cook, covered, on 100% power (high) 5 to 6 minutes or till tender. Turn breasts over after 2½ minutes.

Chicken Pecan Roll-Ups

¼ cup chopped pecans
¼ cup chopped onion
¼ teaspoon ground cumin
1 tablespoon margarine

● In a medium skillet cook pecans, onion, and cumin in margarine till onion is tender and pecans are lightly toasted. Remove from heat.

2 cups chopped cooked chicken
1 3-ounce package cream cheese, cut up
3 tablespoons milk

● Add chicken, cream cheese, milk, and ¼ teaspoon *salt* to the nut mixture in skillet. Heat and stir till well combined.

8 8-inch flour tortillas
1 cup shredded Monterey Jack *or* cheddar cheese
1 large tomato, chopped
½ cup alfalfa sprouts
2 tablespoons pecans

● Spoon about ⅓ *cup* of the mixture onto *each* tortilla. Top with some cheese, tomato, sprouts, and pecans. Roll up and serve. Makes 4 servings.

Nutrition information per serving: 530 calories, 33 g protein, 27 g carbohydrate, 33 g fat, 112 mg cholesterol, 451 mg sodium, 369 mg potassium.

The filling is also delicious baked in bread bundles. Prepare the roll-ups as directed, *except* use refrigerated crescent rolls and omit tortillas, tomato, and sprouts. Unroll crescent dough and separate at perforations to form four rectangles; pat dough to seal perforations. Place some chicken mixture in the center of each rectangle; fold corners over center, pinching edges to seal. Place on a lightly greased baking sheet. Brush with milk. Bake in a 375° oven for 10 to 12 minutes or till golden. Sprinkle with cheese and pecans. Return to oven for 2 to 3 minutes or till cheese melts.

Italian-Style Picnic Sandwich

1 tablespoon Thousand Island salad dressing
1 teaspoon prepared mustard
1 10-ounce package refrigerated pizza dough
3 ounces sliced mozzarella cheese

● Combine salad dressing and mustard. Set aside. On a greased baking sheet unroll the dough . Pat into a 10x12-inch rectangle. Arrange cheese on one lengthwise half of the dough, leaving 1 inch of dough uncovered along 3 sides. Spread *half* of the dressing mixture atop.

6 ounces thinly sliced baked ham
2 ounces sliced provolone *or* Swiss cheese
1 ounce sliced hard salami

● Layer ham, provolone, remaining dressing mixture, and salami atop. Fold other half of dough over layers. Seal edges with tines of a fork. Make slits in top layer.

● Bake in a 400° oven for 18 to 20 minutes. Cover with foil after 10 minutes. Let stand 5 to 10 minutes. Serves 4 to 6.

Nutrition information per serving: 390 calories, 26 g protein, 34 g carbohydrate, 16 g fat, 51 mg cholesterol, 1,296 mg sodium, 258 mg potassium.

There's no reason to get out the condiments— they're already in the sandwich.

Polynesian Chicken Sandwich

1 **8¼-ounce can pineapple slices**	● Drain pineapple, reserving juice. Set pineapple aside. Combine pineapple juice and teriyaki sauce in a shallow dish.
¼ **cup teriyaki sauce**	

4 **skinless, boneless chicken breast halves (¾ pound)**	● Place each chicken breast half between 2 pieces of clear plastic wrap. Using a meat mallet, pound chicken to ¼-inch thickness. Add chicken pieces to teriyaki mixture, turning once to coat. Cover and marinate for 2 to 4 hours in the refrigerator or for 30 minutes at room temperature.

4 **slices Swiss cheese (4 ounces)**	● Remove chicken, reserving marinade. Place chicken on rack of an unheated broiler pan and broil 4 inches from heat for 4 minutes. Baste with reserved marinade. Turn chicken over; broil 3 to 4 minutes more or till no pink remains.
4 **hamburger buns or Kaiser rolls, split**	
1 **cup alfalfa sprouts**	
¼ **cup mayonnaise or salad dressing**	Top each chicken piece with a slice of pineapple and a slice of cheese. Broil about 1 minute or till the cheese melts. Place chicken stacks on buns. Top each sandwich with sprouts and mayonnaise or salad dressing. Makes 4 servings.

Microwave Directions: Marinate chicken as above. Remove chicken, reserving marinade. Place chicken in a 12x7½x2-inch microwave-safe baking dish. Cover with vented clear plastic wrap and cook on 100% power (high) for 3 minutes. Brush with teriyaki sauce; rearrange pieces. Cook on 100% power (high) for 3 to 5 minutes more or till done. Add a pineapple and cheese slice to each chicken piece. Micro-cook on 100% power (high) about 1 minute or till cheese just melts. Serve as above.

Nutrition information per serving: 516 calories, 39 g protein, 35 g carbohydrate, 24 g fat, 109 mg cholesterol, 1,070 mg sodium, 409 mg potassium.

For a flavor twist, instead of the mayonnaise use a sour cream dip, such as bacon and horseradish or French onion, or a creamy salad dressing, such as cucumber or poppy seed.

Hoagie Pocket

Mexican Pizza Pitas

Pocket Joes
(see recipe, page 38)

Mexican Pizza Pitas

¾ **pound ground beef**
1 **small onion, chopped**
1 **teaspoon sugar**
¾ **teaspoon chili powder**
½ **teaspoon garlic salt**

● In a skillet, cook ground beef and onion till meat is brown and onion is tender. Drain well. Stir in sugar, chili powder, and garlic salt.

Preheating the baking sheet or heating the pitas directly on the oven rack makes them extra crispy.

1 **8-ounce bottle salsa**
4 **large *or* 8 small pita bread rounds**
1 **4-ounce can chopped green chilies, drained**
1 **2¼-ounce can sliced ripe olives, drained**
1 **cup shredded Monterey Jack cheese (4 ounces)**

● Spread some of the salsa on each pita. Top with the meat mixture, green chilies, olives, and cheese. Place on preheated baking sheet or directly on oven rack. Bake in a 350° oven for 10 minutes or till pita bread is hot and cheese is melted. Makes 4 servings.

Microwave Directions: In a 1-quart microwave-safe casserole combine the ground beef and onion. Cook on 100% power (high) for 4 to 6 minutes or till no pink remains. Drain. Stir in sugar, chili powder, and garlic salt. Assemble as above. Place *half* of the pitas on a microwave-safe plate. Micro-cook, uncovered, on 100% power (high) for 2 to 3 minutes or till hot and cheese is melted. Repeat with remaining pitas.

Nutrition information per serving: 506 calories, 28 g protein, 42 g carbohydrate, 24 g fat, 79 mg cholesterol, 935 mg sodium, 406 mg potassium.

Hoagie Pocket

6 **to 7 ounces total of salami, turkey, chopped ham, bologna, *and/or* cappicola, thinly sliced**
1½ **ounces mozzarella cheese, sliced**

● Cut meat and cheese slices in half.

When it's too hot to cook, think cold cuts. They're versatile, easy to use, and don't require cooking. By varying the meats and other ingredients in this pocket sandwich, you can invent handfuls of new meals.

2 **large pita bread rounds, halved crosswise**
1 **small onion, thinly sliced and separated into rings**
1 **sliced tomato**
1 **cup shredded lettuce**
2 **tablespoons Italian salad dressing**

● Open each pita half to form a pocket. Divide meat and cheese among pita halves. Top each with onion, tomato, and lettuce. Drizzle each with some of the salad dressing. Makes 4 servings.

Nutrition information per serving: 272 calories, 13 g protein, 21 g carbohydrate, 15 g fat, 31 mg cholesterol, 610 mg sodium, 192 mg potassium.

Ham Sandwiches With Apricot Mustard

⅓ cup apricot preserves
2 tablespoons brown mustard

● For apricot mustard, in a small bowl combine apricot preserves and mustard.

A dab of this apricot mustard will add punch to almost any sandwich. Try it on your own favorite concoctions.

8 slices pumpernickel, rye, or wheat bread
8 ounces thinly sliced cooked ham or turkey
4 ounces thinly sliced Havarti cheese
Spinach or lettuce leaves

● On *one side* of *each* slice of bread, spread about *2 teaspoons* apricot mustard. Put *one-fourth* of the ham or turkey and cheese over the mustard on *half* of the bread slices. Top with spinach or lettuce leaves. Cover with remaining bread slices, mustard-side down. Halve sandwiches. Makes 4 sandwiches.

Nutrition information per serving: 410 calories, 26 g protein, 52 g carbohydrate, 12 g fat, 50 mg cholesterol, 1,387 mg sodium, 380 mg potassium.

Pocket Joes

Pictured on page 36.

¾ pound ground beef
⅓ cup chopped onion
⅓ cup chopped celery

● In a skillet cook ground beef, onion, and celery till meat is brown and onion and celery are tender. Drain well.

Our Pocket Joes aren't so sloppy, thanks to pita bread rounds that keep the filling from falling out. To dress them up even more, add a few alfalfa sprouts on top.

1 8-ounce can pizza sauce
1 teaspoon dry mustard
⅛ teaspoon ground red pepper
1 small zucchini, finely chopped

● Stir in pizza sauce, mustard, and pepper. Bring to boiling. Stir in zucchini; heat through.

2 pita bread rounds, halved crosswise

● Fill each pita half with some of the meat mixture. Makes 4 servings.

Microwave Directions: In a 1½-quart casserole combine crumbled beef, onion, and celery. Micro-cook, covered, on 100% power (high) 4 to 5 minutes or until beef is browned, stirring every 2 minutes. Drain off fat. Stir in pizza sauce, mustard, pepper, and zucchini. Cover and cook on 100% power (high) 2 to 3 minutes or till hot. Serve as above.

Nutrition information per serving: 308 calories, 21 g protein, 16 g carbohydrate, 17 g fat, 71 mg cholesterol, 373 mg sodium, 532 mg potassium.

Veggiewiches

1	8-ounce container soft-style cream cheese
3/4	cup shredded carrot
1/4	cup chopped green pepper
1/4	cup chopped cucumber
1/4	cup chopped onion
1/4	cup sliced celery
1	tablespoon lemon juice
1/4	teaspoon pepper

● In a mixing bowl combine soft-style cream cheese, carrot, green pepper, cucumber, onion, celery, lemon juice, and pepper. Chill, if desired.

Savor summer in a sandwich with this light, creamy spread that's full of garden-fresh goodies. Carrot, green pepper, cucumber, and onion add crunch and color. Serve with soup for a light meal.

| 8 | slices rye *or* pumpernickel bread |
| | Lettuce |

● Spread vegetable mixture on *half* of the rye or pumpernickel bread slices. Top with lettuce and remaining bread slices. Makes 4 sandwiches.

Nutrition information per serving: 345 calories, 9 g protein, 35 g carbohydrate, 20 g fat, 1 mg cholesterol, 439 mg sodium, 339 mg potassium.

Sausage-Pepper Hoagies

| 1 1/4 | pounds Italian sausage links |

● In a large skillet, cover sausage links with water; bring to a boil. Simmer, uncovered, for 15 minutes over low heat. Drain sausages; return to skillet.

Using sweet or mild Italian sausage gives this sandwich plenty of zip. But if you enjoy extra-spicy food, use hot Italian sausage.

1	medium green *or* sweet red pepper, cut into 1-inch squares
1	medium onion, cut into 1-inch squares
1	cup spaghetti sauce
1/2	teaspoon dried sage, crushed, *or* 1 1/2 teaspoons snipped fresh sage

● Add pepper, onion, spaghetti sauce, and sage to skillet. Cover and cook over low heat for 10 minutes or till peppers are tender and sausages are done.

| 4 | hoagie buns, split |
| 3/4 | cup shredded mozzarella *or* provolone cheese (3 ounces) |

● Put sausage and pepper mixture into hoagie buns. Top with shredded cheese. Makes 4 servings.

Nutrition information per serving: 546 calories, 27 g protein, 52 g carbohydrate, 25 g fat, 65 mg cholesterol, 1555 mg sodium, 608 mg potassium.

Berry-Poppy Seed Salad
(see recipe, page 42)

Cool-as-a-Cucumber Salads

Salads are made for summer! They're a refreshing way to add crunch and color to any hot-weather menu. And salads are a perfect way to take advantage of great-tasting fresh fruits and vegetables. Toss or tote them for any occasion, from an easy-to-fix supper for the family to a potluck lunch with friends.

Asparagus Salad
(see recipe, page 43

Curried Pineapple-Orange Salad
(see recipe, page 43)

Marinated Shrimp Salad
(see recipe, page 42)

Marinated Shrimp Salad

Pictured on page 41.

Impress guests with this showy toss-together salad.

1	**16-ounce package frozen peeled and deveined medium shrimp** *or* **1¼ pounds fresh shrimp**
2	**6-ounce jars marinated artichoke hearts**
2	**medium carrots, thinly biased sliced**
¾	**cup sliced celery**
¼	**cup sliced green onion**
¼	**cup sliced pimiento, drained and chopped**

● Cook frozen shrimp according to package directions. (For fresh shrimp, peel, devein, and cook in boiling water about 2 to 3 minutes till shrimp turn pink.) Drain; cool and chill thoroughly.

Drain artichoke hearts, reserving marinade. Cut large pieces of artichoke hearts in half. In a large bowl combine shrimp, artichoke hearts, carrots, celery, green onion, and pimiento.

2	**tablespoons white wine vinegar**
1	**tablespoon sugar**
1	**tablespoon salad oil**
¾	**teaspoon dry mustard**
½	**teaspoon dried oregano, crushed**
½	**teaspoon dried basil, crushed**
1	**clove garlic, minced**
⅛	**teaspoon pepper**

● In a screw-top jar combine the reserved artichoke marinade, vinegar, sugar, salad oil, mustard, oregano, basil, garlic, and pepper. Cover and shake well. Toss with shrimp mixture. Chill 2 to 24 hours before serving.

½	**medium head of red leaf lettuce**
2	**tablespoons snipped parsley (optional)**

● To serve, drain dressing from salad, if desired, and transfer to serving bowl lined with red leaf lettuce. If desired, sprinkle with parsley. Makes 4 servings.

Nutrition information per serving: 325 calories, 26 g protein, 21 g carbohydrate, 16 g fat, 173 mg cholesterol, 417 mg sodium, 726 mg potassium.

Berry-Poppy Seed Salad

Pictured on page 40.

When strawberries aren't available, refreshing green kiwi fruit is a delightful substitute in this salad. For 2 cups, peel and slice four kiwi fruit.

3	**tablespoons salad oil**
3	**tablespoons honey**
1	**tablespoon vinegar**
1	**teaspoon poppy seed**
½	**teaspoon prepared mustard**

● For dressing, in a small bowl combine salad oil, honey, vinegar, poppy seed, and mustard. Mix well.

4	**cups torn Bibb** *or* **Boston lettuce**
2	**cups sliced strawberries** *or* **strawberries** *and* **blueberries**
1	**small onion, thinly sliced and separated into rings**

● In a large salad bowl combine lettuce, berries, and onion. Toss with dressing. Makes 4 servings.

Nutrition information per serving: 188 calories, 1 g protein, 24 g carbohydrate, 11g fat, 0 mg cholesterol, 12 mg sodium, 316 mg potassium.

Curried Pineapple-Orange Salad

Pictured on page 40.

¼ cup cider vinegar
2 tablespoons salad oil
1 teaspoon sugar
1 clove garlic, minced
¼ teaspoon curry powder
¼ teaspoon salt
⅛ teaspoon pepper

● In large bowl combine vinegar, salad oil, sugar, garlic, curry, salt, and pepper.

To eliminate having to peel and section fresh oranges, substitute two 11-ounce cans of mandarin orange sections, drained, for the oranges. Then speed chilling by placing them in the freezer for 20 minutes.

1 20-ounce can pineapple chunks, drained
3 medium oranges, peeled and sectioned
1 small red onion, thinly sliced and separated into rings
6 lettuce leaves
1 medium avocado, cut into slices

● Add pineapple, oranges, and onion. Toss till well coated. Cover and refrigerate 2 to 24 hours.
To serve, spoon fruit mixture with a slotted spoon onto lettuce leaves; garnish with avocado slices. Drizzle with marinade from the bottom of the bowl, if desired. Makes 6 servings.

Nutrition information per serving: 164 calories, 2 g protein, 20 g carbohydrate, 10 g fat, 0 mg cholesterol, 89 mg sodium, 486 mg potassium.

Asparagus Salad

Pictured on page 41.

1 pound fresh asparagus, cut into 1½-inch pieces, *or* two 10-ounce packages frozen asparagus
1 medium carrot, thinly sliced

● In a medium saucepan bring 1 cup *water* to boiling. Add asparagus and carrot. Return water to boiling. Cover and cook for 3 minutes. (For frozen asparagus, cook according to package directions. Add carrot 3 minutes before end of cooking.) Drain and immediately rinse in cold water.

If prosciutto or ham isn't your cup of tea, try bite-size pieces of leftover or deli cooked beef, or cold cuts, such as thinly sliced turkey or chicken.

2 tablespoons soy sauce
1 teaspoon sugar
1 teaspoon vinegar
½ teaspoon sesame oil
⅛ teaspoon pepper
1 cup sliced mushrooms *or* bean sprouts

● Meanwhile, in a small mixing bowl combine soy sauce, sugar, vinegar, sesame oil, and pepper. Place asparagus and carrot in another mixing bowl with mushrooms or bean sprouts. Pour dressing over vegetables. Mix well. Chill 1 to 24 hours.

¼ cup diced prosciutto *or* fully cooked ham
Sliced black olives (optional)
Chopped pimiento (optional)

● Drain vegetables and place in a serving bowl. Add prosciutto or ham and toss to mix. If desired, garnish with black olives and pimiento. Makes 4 servings.

Nutrition information per serving: 71 calories, 7 g protein, 10 g carbohydrate, 1 g fat, 5 mg cholesterol, 636 mg sodium, 484 mg potassium.

Apple-Chicken Salad

¼ cup frozen apple juice concentrate, thawed
2 tablespoons salad oil
2 tablespoons soy sauce
1 tablespoon white wine vinegar
1 teaspoon dried savory, crushed

● For marinade, in a small bowl combine apple juice concentrate, salad oil, soy sauce, vinegar, and savory.

Save time and energy by planning ahead. Get two meals from one by doubling the chicken-marinade mixture. Then broil or grill and serve half for dinner. Chill the rest to use in this salad the next day.

4 medium skinless, boneless chicken breast halves (12 ounces)

● Place chicken breasts in a plastic bag in a shallow dish. Pour marinade over chicken. Close bag. Refrigerate about 4 hours, turning once. Remove meat, reserving marinade. Pat chicken dry with paper towels.
  Place chicken on a rack of an unheated broiler pan. Broil about 4 to 6 inches from heat for 8 to 10 minutes or till tender, brushing occasionally with reserved marinade. (*Or,* grill chicken on an uncovered grill directly over *medium-hot* coals for 20 to 25 minutes or till tender, turning once. Remove from heat. Cut chicken into strips. Cover and chill 2 to 24 hours.

¾ cup mayonnaise *or* salad dressing
¼ cup apple juice concentrate
¼ teaspoon salt
¼ teaspoon pepper

● Meanwhile, for salad dressing, in a small bowl combine mayonnaise or salad dressing, apple juice concentrate, salt, and pepper.

3 cups torn romaine
2 cups torn red leaf lettuce
½ cup broken pecans *or* walnuts
⅓ cup red onion rings
2 medium apples, cored and sliced

● In large bowl combine the romaine, red leaf lettuce, pecans or walnuts, and onion. Divide salad greens among 4 dinner plates. Arrange chicken and apples over greens. Drizzle salad dressing over salads. Makes 4 main-dish salads.

Nutrition information per serving: 705 calories, 31 g protein, 32 g carbohydrate, 52 g fat, 98 mg cholesterol, 959 mg sodium, 782 mg potassium.

Lime-Beef Salad

1	1-pound beef flank *or* top round steak, cut about ½ inch thick	● Place meat on the rack of an unheated broiler pan. Broil 3 inches from heat for 6 minutes. Turn and broil 7 to 8 minutes more for medium-rare. (*Or,* grill steak on an uncovered grill directly over *hot* coals for 12 to 14 minutes or till medium-rare, turning once.) Cool slightly. Slice across the grain into thin, bite-size strips. Place strips in a plastic bag set in a deep bowl.

You'll understand the saying "great things come to those who wait" when you taste this salad. The beef marinates as you enjoy summertime activities and is ready for dinner when you are.

½	cup sliced green onion	● For marinade and dressing, in a bowl mix onion, lime juice, sugar, water, oil, garlic, 1 teaspoon *salt,* and ½ teaspoon *pepper.* Reserve *half* of lime mixture for use as dressing. Pour other half over beef. Close bag; refrigerate for 4 to 24 hours hours. Turn once.
½	cup lime juice	
¼	cup sugar	
¼	cup water	
2	tablespoons salad oil	
4	cloves garlic, minced	

8	cups torn mixed greens	● Divide torn mixed greens among 4 salad plates. Divide pepper and zucchini among the plates. Top with meat mixture. Pass reserved dressing. Makes 4 main-dish servings.
1	medium sweet red *or* green pepper, thinly sliced and separated into rings	
1	small zucchini, cut into julienne strips	

Nutrition information per serving: 360 calories, 25 g protein, 22 g carbohydrate, 20 g fat, 60 mg cholesterol, 635 mg sodium, 902 mg potassium.

Curried Fruity Chicken Salad

1	cup corkscrew macaroni	● Cook macaroni according to package directions. Drain; run under cold water. Drain again.
1	15¼-ounce can pineapple tidbits, drained	
2	cups chopped cooked chicken	In large bowl combine cooked pasta, pineapple, chicken, cantaloupe, grapes, and celery. In a small bowl, combine mayonnaise or salad dressing, curry, and ⅛ teaspoon *salt.* Add to fruit mixture; stir to coat. Cover; chill 2 to 24 hours.
½	medium cantaloupe, cubed	
1	cup seedless green *or* red grapes, halved	
½	cup sliced celery	
½	cup mayonnaise *or* salad dressing	
2	teaspoons curry powder	

Curry powder adds a distinctive bite to this hearty salad. To give it more punch, add a little extra curry.

½	cup peanuts, cashews, *or* chopped walnuts	● To serve, stir in nuts. Serve on salad plates. Makes 4 main-dish servings.

Nutrition information per serving: 653 calories, 31 g protein, 52 g carbohydrate, 37 g fat, 79 mg cholesterol, 383 mg sodium, 870 mg potassium.

Cantaloupe-Chicken Salad

2 **cups fresh peas** *or* **one 10-ounce package frozen peas**	● Cook fresh peas, covered, in a small amount of boiling water 10 to 12 minutes or just till tender. (Or, place frozen peas in a colander and run cold water over them to thaw.) Drain. In a large mixing bowl combine peas, chicken, and green onion. Set aside.
2 **cups chopped cooked chicken**	
⅓ **cup sliced green onion**	

Hint: If you're short on time, just quarter the cantaloupe instead of slicing it.

⅔ **cup watercress, finely chopped**	● For dressing, in a small bowl combine watercress, mayonnaise or salad dressing, sour cream, lemon peel, Dijon-style mustard, and pepper. Stir into chicken mixture. Cover and chill 2 to 24 hours.
½ **cup mayonnaise** *or* **salad dressing**	
½ **cup dairy sour cream**	
1 **teaspoon shredded lemon peel**	
1 **teaspoon Dijon-style mustard**	
¼ **teaspoon pepper**	

Watercress, Bibb lettuce, *or* **endive**	● To assemble, line 4 plates with watercress, lettuce, or endive. Arrange cantaloupe slices atop. Add chicken mixture. Makes 4 main-dish servings.
1 **medium cantaloupe, halved, seeded, and thinly sliced**	

Nutrition information per serving: 474 calories, 25 g protein, 18 g carbohydrate, 34 g fat, 92 mg cholesterol, 297 mg sodium, 852 mg potassium.

Herbed Cottage Cheese Salad

1 **12-ounce carton cottage cheese**	● In a bowl combine cottage cheese, sour cream, cucumber, green pepper, onion, basil, pepper, and tarragon.
½ **cup dairy sour cream**	
½ **cup chopped cucumber**	
½ **cup chopped green pepper**	
1 **sliced green onion**	
⅛ **teaspoon dried basil, crushed**	
⅛ **teaspoon pepper**	
⅛ **teaspoon dried tarragon, crushed**	

Dress up the old standby, cottage cheese, by teaming it with crisp fresh vegetables and a medley of herbs.

4 **lettuce leaves**	● Serve cottage cheese mixture on lettuce-lined plates. Top with vegetable strips. Makes 4 main-dish servings.
16 **strips of celery, carrot, green** *or* **sweet red pepper,** *or* **unpeeled zucchini**	

Nutrition information per serving: 183 calories, 13 g protein, 10 g carbohydrate, 10 g fat, 26 mg cholesterol, 391 mg sodium, 431 mg potassium.

Primavera Salad
(see recipe, page 52)

Herbed Chicken
(see recipe, page 51)

NATIONAL

NATIO

BAI

CI

Food for a Crowd

Whether it's for a day at the balloon races, beach, ballpark, or in the backyard, this savory picnic menu for 6 or 12 is portable, yet elegant. Make everything ahead, pack it up, and then sit back and enjoy the food, fun, and fresh air. For more ideas on feeding a crowd, see the recipes on the following pages—all are sized to take the guesswork out of feeding up to 12 people.

Berry-Glazed Picnic Cake
(see recipe, page 53)

Hold-the-Ants! Picnic

Menu

Herbed Chicken
Hard rolls and butter
Primavera Salad *or*
    Medley Salad
Berry-Glazed Picnic Cake
Soda water *or* wine

Menu Countdown

Up to 24 Hours Ahead:
Prepare Herbed Chicken. Cover and refrigerate at least 4 hours.
Prepare Primavera Salad or Medley Salad. Cover salad and refrigerate for at least 4 hours.
Prepare Berry-Glazed Picnic Cake without topping; cool and then refrigerate.

Up to 3 Hours Ahead:
Thinly slice chilled chicken breasts. Pack in a covered container or wrap in foil.
Top baked and chilled cake with fresh strawberry slices, melted jelly, and almonds. Cut into serving-size pieces. Pack in a covered container or cover with plastic wrap.

Chill soda water or wine, if necessary.
Keep cold foods covered in the refrigerator until you leave.
Fill a picnic basket with a blanket; plates; flatware; napkins; salt and pepper shakers; serving utensils; a bottle opener or corkscrew, if needed; glasses; and paper towels.

Just Before You Go:
Pack butter into a small airtight container, and hard rolls in a plastic bag.
To transport, pack well-chilled food into an insulated cooler with ice packs or block ice.

At Serving Time:
Lightly toss salad.

After Serving:
Promptly return leftovers to the insulated cooler.

Herbed Chicken

Pictured on page 48.

6 SERVINGS

| | **12 SERVINGS** |

½ teaspoon salt
½ teaspoon paprika
¼ teaspoon pepper
6 medium skinless, boneless chicken breast halves
2 tablespoons cooking oil

● In a custard cup combine salt, paprika, and pepper. Sprinkle on both sides of each chicken breast half.
 In a 12-inch skillet cook chicken breasts in oil, uncovered, over medium heat till brown, turning once.

1 teaspoon salt
1 teaspoon paprika
½ teaspoon pepper
12 medium skinless, boneless chicken breast halves
2 to 3 tablespoons cooking oil

⅓ cup chicken broth
⅓ cup dry white wine
1 tablespoon snipped fresh basil *or* 1 teaspoon dried basil, crushed

● Add broth, wine, and basil to skillet. Cook, covered, over medium-low heat for 10 minutes or till just tender. Cover; refrigerate 4 to 24 hours. To serve, thinly slice.
 To transport, pack well-chilled chicken slices into an insulated cooler with ice packs or block ice.

Nutrition information per serving: 195 calories, 27 g protein, 1 g carbohydrate, 8 g fat, 72 mg cholesterol, 287 mg sodium, 255 mg potassium.

½ cup chicken broth
½ cup dry white wine
2 tablespoons snipped fresh basil *or* 2 teaspoons dried basil, crushed

Medley Salad

6 SERVINGS

| | **12 SERVINGS** |

4 ounces fresh green beans, cut into 1½-inch pieces (1 cup)
1 cup sliced carrots

● Cook beans, in boiling salted water, covered, for 5 minutes. Add carrots. Cook 7 to 9 minutes more or till crisp-tender. Rinse vegetables under cold water and drain.

8 ounces fresh green beans, cut into 1½-inch pieces (2 cups)
2 cups sliced carrots

2 medium green *and/or* sweet red peppers, cut into ½-inch squares
1 small summer squash, thinly sliced
½ cup whole pitted ripe olives
¼ cup vinegar
2 tablespoons salad oil
2 cloves garlic, minced
½ teaspoon dried oregano, crushed
½ cup coarsely crumbled feta cheese

● In a large mixing bowl combine drained, cooked beans and carrots with peppers, summer squash, and olives.
 In a screw-top jar combine vinegar, oil, garlic, and oregano. Shake well. Toss with salad. Top with cheese. Cover; refrigerate 4 to 24 hours. Stir salad before serving.
 To transport, pack well-chilled salad into an insulated cooler with ice packs or block ice.

Nutrition information per serving: 88 calories, 1 g protein, 7 g carbohydrate, 7 g fat, 0 mg cholesterol, 91 mg sodium, 233 mg potassium.

4 medium green *and/or* sweet red peppers, cut into ½-inch squares
2 small summer squash, thinly sliced
1 cup whole pitted ripe olives
½ cup vinegar
¼ cup salad oil
4 cloves garlic, minced
1 teaspoon dried oregano, crushed
1 cup coarsely crumbled feta cheese

Primavera Salad

Pictured on page 48.

6 SERVINGS / **12 SERVINGS**

6 SERVINGS		12 SERVINGS
1 **7-ounce package refrigerated *or* frozen cheese-filled tortellini (2 cups)** 1 **medium sweet red *or* green pepper, cut into thin bite-size strips** 1 **cup broccoli flowerets** 1 **medium carrot, thinly sliced** ⅓ **cup sliced pitted ripe olives**	● Cook tortellini according to package directions; drain. Rinse with cold water; drain well. In a large mixing bowl combine tortellini, pepper, broccoli, carrot, and olives.	2 **7-ounce packages refrigerated *or* frozen cheese-filled tortellini (4 cups)** 2 **medium sweet red *or* green peppers, cut into thin bite-size strips** 2 **cups broccoli flowerets** 2 **medium carrots, thinly sliced** ⅔ **cup sliced pitted ripe olives**
⅓ **cup mayonnaise *or* salad dressing** ⅓ **cup purchased pesto *or* Homemade Pesto (see recipe, below)** ¼ **cup milk** ¼ **teaspoon pepper**	● For dressing, in a small mixing bowl stir together mayonnaise or salad dressing, pesto, milk, and pepper. Pour dressing over tortellini mixture; toss till combined.	⅔ **cup mayonnaise *or* salad dressing** ⅔ **cup purchased pesto *or* Homemade Pesto (see recipe, below)** ½ **cup milk** ½ **teaspoon pepper**
Fresh spinach leaves (optional)	● Cover and chill 4 to 24 hours. If desired, serve in a spinach-lined bowl. To transport, pack well-chilled salad into an insulated cooler with ice packs or block ice.	**Fresh spinach leaves (optional)**

Nutrition information per serving: 287 calories, 8 g protein, 22 g carbohydrate, 19 g fat, 28 mg cholesterol, 372 mg sodium, 329 mg potassium.

Homemade Pesto

Pesto, an herb paste used to enhance the flavor of pasta and other dishes, is the perfect way to feature fresh basil and parsley.

To make pesto, rinse herbs and pick the leaves from the stems. Place *2 cups* lightly packed leaves and two cloves *garlic* into your food processor or blender. Cover; process or blend till finely chopped. Stop the processor or blender several times to scrape down the sides so everything gets chopped. Now add ¾ cup *grated Parmesan or Romano cheese*. Once again, process or blend till combined. Finally, gradually add ½ cup *olive or cooking oil*, processing or blending well the entire time.

Berry-Glazed Picnic Cake

Pictured on page 49.

6 SERVINGS

½ cup all-purpose flour
2 tablespoons sugar
1 teaspoon finely shredded lemon peel
½ teaspoon baking powder
¼ cup margarine *or* butter, softened
1 egg yolk, beaten
2 tablespoons milk
¼ teaspoon vanilla

1 8-ounce package *and* one 3-ounce package cream cheese, softened
1 cup sugar
2 egg yolks
1 teaspoon vanilla
2 teaspoons lemon juice

2 cups fresh strawberries, sliced
¼ cup currant jelly
2 tablespoons sliced almonds, toasted

12 SERVINGS

1 cup all-purpose flour
¼ cup sugar
2 teaspoons finely shredded lemon peel
1 teaspoon baking powder
½ cup margarine *or* butter, softened
1 egg, beaten
¼ cup milk
½ teaspoon vanilla

2 8-ounce packages *and* one 3-ounce package cream cheese, softened
1¼ cups sugar
1 egg
2 teaspoons vanilla
1 tablespoon lemon juice

4 cups fresh strawberries, sliced
½ cup currant jelly
¼ cup sliced almonds, toasted

● For bottom layer, in a medium mixing bowl stir together flour, sugar, lemon peel, and baking powder. Cut in margarine or butter till mixture resembles coarse crumbs. Make a well in the center.

In a small bowl combine egg yolk or egg, milk, and vanilla; add all at once to flour mixture. Stir just till dough clings together. Spread into bottom of an 8x8x2-inch baking pan. (For 12 servings, use a 13x9x2-inch baking pan.)

● For cheese layer, in a small mixer bowl, combine cream cheese, sugar, egg yolks or egg, vanilla, and lemon juice. Beat on high speed till smooth and creamy. Spread over the dough in the pan. Bake in a 350° oven for 30 to 35 minutes or till top is golden. Cool completely on a wire rack. Cover and refrigerate 4 to 24 hours.

● Not more than 3 hours before serving, arrange strawberry slices atop cake. Stir jelly to soften; brush over berries. Sprinkle with almonds. Chill.

To transport, pack well-chilled cake into an insulated cooler with ice packs or block ice.

Nutrition information per serving: 524 calories, 7 g protein, 60 g carbohydrate, 30 g fat, 164 mg cholesterol, 278 mg sodium, 204 mg potassium.

Picnic Pointers

Outdoor eating is part of the fun of summer. To ensure that your food is as tasty and fresh at the picnic site as it was before you set out, keep these hints in mind.

● When planning for warm-weather outings, opt for foods that are the least likely to spoil, such as breads, hard cheeses, chilled hard-cooked eggs (in the shell), canned meats, baked beans, marinated salads, and fresh fruits and vegetables.

● Keep all work surfaces, utensils, and your hands immaculate during food preparation so harmful bacteria won't be transferred to the picnic foods. Use bottled mayonnaise or salad dressing rather than homemade for salads and sandwiches. The acidity of commercial mayonnaise helps prevent spoilage.

● Make sure all meat is thoroughly cooked and chilled. Always refrigerate meat as soon as it is cooked. Don't wait for it to cool to room temperature before refrigerating.

● Put tightly wrapped and well-chilled fried chicken, baked ham, and raw meats for grilling in the bottom of the cooler. Pack your cooler so the food to be eaten first is on top. This way you avoid unpacking and repacking the food outdoors. Use ice packs or blocks of ice because they last longer than ice cubes. Avoid dry ice because it causes freezer burn to food and bare skin.

● Keep sandwiches from becoming soggy by packing lettuce and condiments in separate containers. Add them to sandwiches just before serving.

● Avoid soggy tossed salads by packing salad dressings in separate containers with tight-fitting lids. Place salad ingredients in big plastic bags or bowls. Toss just before eating.

● To transport cupcakes, split each in half; spread icing on the inside. This way the icing won't stick to the plastic wrap.

● Fill ice cube trays with some of your picnic beverage, then freeze. Just before leaving home, add these to your beverage jug instead of ice cubes. Or, purchase drinks in individual cartons and freeze them. Packed in a cooler, they'll keep other foods cold and will be thawed by picnic time.

● Tape the tops of salt and pepper shakers to avoid spills while transporting them.

● Urge everyone to bring along a hearty appetite to eliminate leftovers. Don't carry home leftovers—discard them. Any food that has been exposed to sunshine or warm temperatures can be harmful, even though it may still look appetizing.

Deviled Eggs

6 SERVINGS		12 SERVINGS
3 eggs	● To hard-cook eggs, place in a large saucepan; add enough water to cover. Bring to boiling; reduce heat to just below simmering. Cover; cook for 15 minutes. Remove from heat. Drain. Fill saucepan with cold water (see photo, below). Drain. Remove shells. Cut eggs in half lengthwise. Remove yolks; place in mixing bowl. Set whites aside.	**6 eggs**
2 tablespoons mayonnaise **½ teaspoon prepared mustard** **¼ teaspoon dried parsley flakes** **¼ teaspoon Worcestershire sauce** **⅛ teaspoon onion powder** **⅛ teaspoon pepper**	● Mash yolks with a fork. Add mayonnaise, mustard, parsley, Worcestershire sauce, onion powder, and pepper. Mix with a fork till combined.	**¼ cup mayonnaise** **1 teaspoon prepared mustard** **½ teaspoon dried parsley flakes** **½ teaspoon Worcestershire sauce** **¼ teaspoon onion powder** **¼ teaspoon pepper**
Pimiento-stuffed olives _or_ cooked bacon, crumbled (optional) **Paprika**	● Fill reserved egg whites with yolk mixture (see photo, below). If desired, garnish with olives or bacon. Sprinkle with paprika. Cover and refrigerate up to 24 hours. To transport, pack well-chilled eggs into an insulated cooler with ice packs or block ice. Nutrition information per serving: 74 calories, 3 g protein, 1 g carbohydrate, 7 g fat, 140 mg cholesterol, 69 mg sodium, 40 mg potassium.	**Pimiento-stuffed olives _or_ cooked bacon, crumbled (optional)** **Paprika**

For hard-cooked eggs with few rings, cool the eggs quickly. If your tap water isn't icy cold, add ice cubes to the pan of eggs after you've cooled them with tap water.

To fill egg whites, spoon egg yolk mixture into centers. Or, for a decorative touch, pipe the egg yolk mixture into the cavities of the egg whites using a decorating bag fitted with a large star tip.

Traditional
Potato Salad

Traditional Potato Salad

6 SERVINGS		12 SERVINGS
4 **medium potatoes (1⅓ pounds)**	● In a large saucepan cook potatoes in boiling salted water, covered, for 20 to 25 minutes or till tender. Drain. Cool slightly. Peel and cube; transfer to a large mixing bowl.	8 **medium potatoes (2⅔ pounds)**
2 **hard-cooked eggs, coarsely chopped** ½ **cup thinly sliced celery** ¼ **cup chopped onion *or* sliced green onion** ¼ **cup finely shredded carrot** ¼ **cup chopped sweet pickle *or* sweet pickle relish**	● Add eggs, celery, onion, carrot, and sweet pickle or relish to potatoes.	4 **hard-cooked eggs, coarsely chopped** 1 **cup thinly sliced celery** ½ **cup chopped onion *or* sliced green onion** ½ **cup finely shredded carrot** ½ **cup chopped sweet pickle *or* sweet pickle relish**
⅔ **cup mayonnaise *or* salad dressing** 2 **teaspoons prepared mustard** ½ **teaspoon celery seed** ½ **teaspoon salt** **Leaf lettuce (optional)** 1 **hard-cooked egg, sliced (optional)** ¼ **teaspoon paprika (optional)**	● For dressing, in a mixing bowl combine mayonnaise or salad dressing, prepared mustard, celery seed, and salt. Add mayonnaise mixture to potatoes. Toss lightly to coat potato mixture. Cover and chill 4 to 24 hours. If desired, serve in a lettuce-lined bowl and garnish with egg slices and paprika. To transport, pack well-chilled salad into an insulated cooler with ice packs or block ice.	1¼ **cups mayonnaise *or* salad dressing** 1 **tablespoon prepared mustard** 1 **teaspoon celery seed** ¾ **teaspoon salt** **Leaf lettuce (optional)** 1 **hard-cooked egg, sliced (optional)** ½ **teaspoon paprika (optional)**

Nutrition information per serving: 296 calories, 5 g protein, 22 g carbohydrate, 22 g fat, 106 mg cholesterol, 451 mg sodium, 601 mg potassium.

Hot Mustard Potato Salad

Vinaigrette
Potato Salad

Vinaigrette Potato Salad

6 SERVINGS		12 SERVINGS
1 pound tiny new potatoes	● Cook potatoes in boiling salted water, covered, for 15 to 20 minutes or till tender. Drain well. When cool enough to handle, quarter potatoes.	2 pounds tiny new potatoes
1 medium green pepper, chopped 1 medium carrot, shredded ¼ cup chopped red onion ¼ cup wine vinegar 2 tablespoons olive *or* salad oil 2 teaspoons sugar ½ teaspoon garlic salt ½ teaspoon dry mustard ⅛ teaspoon pepper	● In a large bowl combine green pepper, carrot, and red onion. Stir in potatoes. In a screw-top jar combine vinegar, oil, sugar, garlic salt, mustard, and pepper. Cover; shake well. Pour over potato mixture, tossing to coat. Cover; refrigerate 4 to 24 hours. To transport, pack well-chilled salad into an insulated cooler with ice packs or block ice. Nutrition information per serving: 126 calories, 2 g protein, 20 g carbohydrate, 5 g fat, 0 mg cholesterol, 162 mg sodium, 386 mg potassium.	2 medium green peppers, chopped 2 medium carrots, shredded ½ cup chopped red onion ½ cup wine vinegar ¼ cup olive *or* salad oil 4 teaspoons sugar 1 teaspoon garlic salt 1 teaspoon dry mustard ¼ teaspoon pepper

Hot Mustard Potato Salad

6 SERVINGS		12 SERVINGS
6 medium potatoes (2 pounds)	● Cook potatoes in boiling salted water, covered, about 25 minutes or till tender. Drain well. Peel and slice.	12 medium potatoes (4 pounds)
6 slices bacon ½ cup chopped onion 1 tablespoon sugar 1 tablespoon all-purpose flour 1 tablespoon prepared mustard ⅔ cup water ¼ cup vinegar 2 tablespoons snipped parsley	● Cook bacon till crisp. Drain; reserving *2 tablespoons* drippings in skillet. Crumble bacon; set aside. Add onion to skillet and cook till tender. Stir in sugar, flour, and mustard. Add the water and vinegar. Stir till smooth. Cook and stir till thickened and bubbly. Stir in bacon and potatoes. Cook about 5 minutes or till hot, tossing lightly. Remove from heat. Toss with parsley. Serve at once. (Do not transport.) Nutrition information per serving: 188 calories, 5 g protein, 35 g carbohydrate, 3 g fat, 5 mg cholesterol, 118 mg sodium, 645 mg potassium.	12 slices bacon 1 cup chopped onion 2 tablespoons sugar 2 tablespoons all-purpose flour 2 tablespoons prepared mustard 1⅓ cups water ½ cup vinegar ¼ cup snipped parsley

New Red Potato Salad

6 SERVINGS

1½ pounds tiny new potatoes (12 to 15) *or* red potatoes, cut into bite-size pieces

½ cup plain low-fat yogurt
½ cup chopped green pepper
¼ cup chopped onion
¼ cup chopped dill pickle
2 tablespoons sliced black olives
2 tablespoons chopped pimiento
1 teaspoon snipped fresh tarragon *or* ¼ teaspoon dried tarragon, crushed
½ teaspoon salt
⅛ teaspoon pepper

● In a large saucepan cook potatoes in boiling salted water, covered, for 13 to 15 minutes till tender but firm. Drain potatoes well.

● For dressing, in a large mixing bowl combine yogurt, green pepper, onion, dill pickle, olives, pimiento, tarragon, salt, and pepper. Toss potatoes with dressing till coated. Cover and chill for 4 to 24 hours.

To transport, pack well-chilled salad into an insulated cooler with ice packs or block ice.

Nutrition information per serving: 125 calories, 3 g protein, 27 g carbohydrate, 1 g fat, 1 mg cholesterol, 320 mg sodium, 527 mg potassium.

12 SERVINGS

3 pounds tiny new potatoes (24 to 30) *or* red potatoes, cut into bite-size pieces

1 8-ounce container plain low-fat yogurt
1 cup chopped green pepper
½ cup chopped onion
½ cup chopped dill pickle
¼ cup sliced black olives
1 2-ounce jar chopped pimiento
2 teaspoons snipped fresh tarragon *or* ½ teaspoon dried tarragon, crushed
1 teaspoon salt
¼ teaspoon pepper

One Potato, Two Potato

What types of potatoes are best for potato salad? In general, round potatoes with firm, waxy interiors are best, especially the red varieties. New potatoes work well, too. They're simply tiny, round potatoes.

How many do you need? Figure about one medium potato per person. Three medium potatoes should weigh about one pound. For new potatoes, plan on six to eight potatoes to the pound and about three potatoes per person.

New Red Potato Salad

Easy-Does-It Potato Salad

6 SERVINGS

12 SERVINGS

½ of a 24-ounce package frozen hash brown potatoes with onion and peppers
¾ cup thinly sliced celery

● In a saucepan cook potatoes with onion and peppers in about 1 inch of boiling water, covered, for 8 to 10 minutes or till potatoes are tender. Drain well. In a 1½-quart casserole combine cooked potatoes and celery. (If making 12 servings use a 2-quart casserole.) Set aside.

1 24-ounce package frozen hash brown potatoes with onion and peppers
1½ cups thinly sliced celery

½ of an 8-ounce container sour cream dip with chives
⅓ cup mayonnaise *or* salad dressing
1½ teaspoons sugar
1½ teaspoons white wine vinegar *or* cider vinegar
½ teaspoon dried dillweed
¼ teaspoon salt
⅛ teaspoon pepper
2 hard-cooked eggs, coarsely chopped

● For dressing, in a small bowl combine sour cream dip, mayonnaise or salad dressing, sugar, vinegar, dill-weed, salt, and pepper. Add mayonnaise mixture to potato mixture; toss lightly to coat. Fold in eggs. Cover; chill for 4 to 24 hours.

1 8-ounce container sour cream dip with chives
⅔ cup mayonnaise *or* salad dressing
1 tablespoon sugar
1 tablespoon white wine vinegar *or* cider vinegar
1 teaspoon dried dillweed
¾ teaspoon salt
¼ teaspoon pepper
4 hard-cooked eggs, coarsely chopped

1 cup halved cherry tomatoes *or* coarsely chopped, seeded tomato
Parsley sprigs (optional)

● Before serving, fold in tomatoes. If desired, garnish with parsley sprigs.
   To transport, pack well-chilled salad into an insulated cooler with ice packs or block ice.

Nutrition information per serving: 279 calories, 5 g protein, 19 g carbohydrate, 22 g fat, 107 mg cholesterol, 269 mg sodium, 374 mg potassium.

2 cups halved cherry tomatoes *or* coarsely chopped, seeded tomato
Parsley sprigs (optional)

Easy-Does-It Potato Salad

Feeding The Gang

If a hungry crowd is coming over, don't panic. We have some ideas to make entertaining the gang fun and hassle-free. Just take a look at some of the simple side dishes on the following pages. Team them with hot dogs or burgers, and you have a meal.

If you want something other than hot dogs or burgers as a main dish, here are some suggestions for easy crowd-size entrées.

● Grill your favorite type of sausage, such as bratwurst, Italian sausage, or kielbasa. Serve in hot dog buns or hoagie rolls with all the condiments.

● When it's too hot to use your oven, use a covered grill for a large roast or whole turkey. Once you start the meat, it can cook unattended, leaving you free for other meal preparations or just to enjoy the day.

● Instead of making several sandwiches, save time and energy by making one large hoagie-style sandwich using a long loaf of French, Italian, or Vienna bread, and a variety of cold cuts. Then, slice it into servings. Or, better yet, provide a selection of buns, pita bread, croissants, cold cuts, and cheeses and let guests create their own sandwiches.

Marinated Bean Salad

6 SERVINGS

½ cup vinegar
¼ cup salad oil
¼ cup sugar

1 15-ounce can garbanzo beans, drained
1 8-ounce can cut wax beans, drained
1 8-ounce can red kidney beans, drained
½ cup coarsely chopped green pepper
½ cup coarsely shredded carrot
3 green onions, sliced

● In a screw-top jar combine vinegar, oil, and sugar; cover and shake well.

● In a large mixing bowl combine the garbanzo beans, wax beans, kidney beans, green pepper, carrot, and onions. Pour vinegar mixture over vegetables and stir lightly. Cover and refrigerate 6 to 24 hours, stirring occasionally. Drain before serving.

To transport, pack well-chilled salad into an insulated cooler with ice packs or block ice.

Nutrition information per serving: 141 calories, 6 g protein, 22 g carbohydrate, 4 g fat, 0 mg cholesterol, 61 mg sodium, 337 mg potassium.

12 SERVINGS

1 cup vinegar
½ cup salad oil
½ cup sugar

2 15-ounce cans garbanzo beans, drained
1 16-ounce can cut wax beans, drained
1 15½-ounce can red kidney beans, drained
1 cup coarsely chopped green pepper
1 cup coarsely shredded carrot
6 green onions, sliced

Coleslaw

6 SERVINGS		12 SERVINGS
½ **cup mayonnaise** *or* **salad dressing** ¼ **cup milk** 2 **tablespoons sugar** 1 **tablespoon vinegar** ¼ **teapoon garlic powder** ¼ **teaspoon onion powder** ¼ **teaspoon dry mustard** ¼ **teaspoon celery salt** **Dash pepper**	● In a mixing bowl combine mayonnaise or salad dressing, milk, sugar, vinegar, garlic powder, onion powder, dry mustard, celery salt, and pepper. Stir till smooth.	1 **cup mayonnaise** *or* **salad dressing** ½ **cup milk** ¼ **cup sugar** 2 **tablespoons vinegar** ½ **teaspoon garlic powder** ½ **teaspoon onion powder** ½ **teaspoon dry mustard** ½ **teaspoon celery salt** ⅛ **teaspoon pepper**
5 **cups finely shredded cabbage** 1 **cup shredded carrot**	● Combine cabbage and carrot. Toss mayonnaise and cabbage mixtures till well coated. Chill 1 to 24 hours. To transport, pack well-chilled salad into an insulated cooler with ice packs or block ice.	10 **cups finely shredded cabbage** 2 **cups shredded carrot**

Nutrition information per serving: 181 calories, 2 g protein, 11 g carbohydrate, 15 g fat, 12 mg cholesterol, 203 mg sodium, 248 mg potassium.

Nut-Topped Snack Cake

6 SERVINGS		12 SERVINGS
½ **cup all-purpose flour** ½ **teaspoon baking powder** ⅛ **teaspoon salt** 1 **egg** ½ **cup sugar** ¼ **cup milk** 2 **tablespoons margarine** *or* **butter**	● Grease and lightly flour an 8-inch round baking pan (6 servings) or a 13x9x2-inch baking pan (12 servings). Combine flour, baking powder, and salt. In a bowl beat egg(s) with electric mixer on high speed for 4 minutes or till thick. Gradually add sugar; beat at medium speed 4 to 5 minutes or till fluffy. Add dry ingredients to egg mixture; stir just till combined. Heat milk with margarine till margarine melts; stir into batter and mix well.	1 **cup all-purpose flour** 1 **teaspoon baking powder** ¼ **teaspoon salt** 2 **eggs** 1 **cup sugar** ½ **cup milk** ¼ **cup margarine** *or* **butter**
⅓ **cup chopped walnuts** *or* **pecans** 2 **tablespoons sugar**	● Pour batter into prepared pan. Combine nuts and sugar; sprinkle evenly over batter. Bake in a 350° oven about 20 minutes or till cake springs back when pressed. Cool in pan. Cut into pieces.	⅔ **cup chopped walnuts** *or* **pecans** ⅓ **cup sugar**

Nutrition information per serving: 109 calories, 2 g protein, 16 g carbohydrate, 5 g fat, 23 mg cholesterol, 65 mg sodium, 36 mg potassium.

Bean Quartet

6 SERVINGS

1 cup chopped onion
6 slices bacon, cut into
   1-inch pieces

1 16-ounce can garbanzo
   beans, drained
1 8-ounce can lima beans,
   drained
1 8-ounce can pork and
   beans with tomato
   sauce
1 8-ounce can red kidney
   beans, drained
½ cup packed brown sugar
½ cup catsup
¼ cup vinegar

● In a skillet cook onion and bacon till bacon is crisp and onion is tender, but not brown; drain.

● In a 1½-quart casserole combine onion mixture, garbanzo beans, lima beans, pork and beans, kidney beans, brown sugar, catsup, and vinegar. Bake, covered, in a 375° oven for 1 hour. Uncover and bake about 10 minutes more or till of desired consistency.

Nutrition information per serving: 175 calories, 7 g protein, 30 g carbohydrate, 3 g fat, 5 mg cholesterol, 358 mg sodium, 373 mg potassium.

12 SERVINGS

2 cups chopped onion
12 slices bacon, cut into
   1-inch pieces

2 16-ounce cans garbanzo
   beans, drained
1 16- *or* 17-ounce can lima
   beans, drained
1 16-ounce can pork and
   beans with tomato
   sauce
1 15-ounce can red kidney
   beans, drained
1 cup packed brown sugar
1 cup catsup
½ cup vinegar

Easy Picnic Baked Beans

6 SERVINGS

1 31-ounce can pork and
   beans in tomato sauce
1 cup chopped onion
½ cup chopped green pepper
¼ cup chili sauce
2 tablespoons molasses
2 teaspoons prepared
   mustard

● In a 1½-quart casserole (3-quart for 12 servings) combine pork and beans*, onion, green pepper, chili sauce, molasses, and mustard.

12 SERVINGS

2 31-ounce cans pork and
   beans in tomato
   sauce
2 cups chopped onion
1 cup chopped green
   pepper
½ cup chili sauce
¼ cup molasses
1 tablespoon prepared
   mustard

● Bake in a 350° oven about 1 hour (1½ hours for 12 servings) or till of desired consistency.

*__Note:__ For 12 servings drain off ⅓ cup liquid from beans.

Nutrition information per serving: 219 calories, 10 g protein, 37 g carbohydrate, 4 g fat, 6 mg cholesterol, 842 mg sodium, 488 mg potassium.

Maple Beans

6 SERVINGS

2 15-ounce cans navy beans
   or great northern beans
3 slices bacon, chopped *or* ¼
   cup diced salt pork
½ cup chopped onion

● Drain beans, reserving liquid.
   In a medium skillet cook bacon or salt pork and onion till onion is tender. Drain on paper towels.

12 SERVINGS

4 15-ounce cans navy
   beans *or* great
   northern beans
6 slices bacon, chopped,
   or ½ cup diced salt
   pork
1 cup chopped onion

½ cup catsup
¼ cup maple syrup
2 tablespoons packed brown
   sugar
1 teaspoon dry mustard
¼ teaspoon pepper

● In a 1-quart casserole (2-quart for 12 servings) combine the beans and the bacon mixture. Stir in *¼ cup (⅓ cup* for 12 servings) of the reserved bean liquid, the catsup, maple syrup, brown sugar, dry mustard, and pepper.

1 cup catsup
½ cup maple syrup
¼ cup packed brown sugar
2 teaspoons dry mustard
½ teaspoon pepper

● Bake, uncovered, in a 350° oven about 1¼ hours or till of desired consistency, stirring occasionally. If necessary, add additional reserved bean liquid.

Nutrition information per serving: 223 calories, 9 g protein, 42 g carbohydrate, 3 g fat, 3 mg cholesterol, 302 mg sodium, 477 mg potassium.

Make-Ahead Lemonade Base *Pictured on page 65.*

2½ cups water 1¼ cups sugar	● In a medium saucepan heat and stir water and sugar over medium heat till sugar dissolves. Remove from heat and cool 20 minutes.
½ teaspoon finely shredded lemon peel 1¼ cups lemon juice	● Add lemon peel and juice to sugar syrup. Pour into a covered jar and refrigerate. (Base can be stored in the refrigerator up to 3 days.)
Cold water Ice 1 lemon, thinly sliced	● For each serving, pour ½ cup base into a glass. Stir in ½ cup water. Fill the glass with ice and garnish with a lemon slice. Makes ten (8-ounce) servings.

This base is great for parties when refrigerator space is limited. Just make it ahead. Then, add water and ice to serve.

Pictured clockwise from lower left: Raspberry Sparkler, *(see recipe, page 66)*; **Piña Colada Flip,** *(see recipe, page 66)*; **Mint Cooler,** *(see recipe, page 66)*; **Tropical Cooler; Razzle-Dazzle Lemonade; Berry Slush,** *(see recipe, page 67)*.

Nutrition information per serving: 69 calories, 0 g protein, 18 g carbohydrate, 0 g fat, 0 mg cholesterol, 0 mg sodium, 26 mg potassium.

Razzle-Dazzle Lemonade: Prepare lemonade base as above. Chill. For each serving, place 1 scoop *lemon sherbet* in a tall glass. Pour ½ *cup* lemonade base and ½ cup *carbonated water* over sherbet. Add a generous tablespoon of fresh *raspberries* or *blueberries*.

Nutrition information per serving: 213 calories, 1 g protein, 50 g carbohydrate, 2 g fat, 7 mg cholesterol, 45 mg sodium, 132 mg potassium.

Tropical Cooler: Prepare lemonade base as above. Chill. For each serving, place ¼ *cup* lemonade base, ¼ cup *orange juice*, and 2 teaspoons *instant tea* in tall glass with *ice*. Add *half* of a 12-ounce can *lemon-lime carbonated beverage*. Garnish with *orange slices*.

Nutrition information per serving: 152 calories, 0 g protein, 39 g carbohydrate, 0 g fat, 0 mg cholesterol, 1 mg sodium, 194 mg potassium.

Lemony Wine Spritzer: Prepare lemonade base as above. Chill. For each serving, place a *lemon slice* in a tall glass. Add *ice cubes*. Pour in ½ *cup* lemonade base and ½ cup chilled *white wine*.

Nutrition information per serving: 171 calories, 0 g protein, 24 g carbohydrate, 0 g fat, 0 mg cholesterol, 6 mg sodium, 134 mg potassium.

Raspberry Sparkler

Pictured on page 65.

1	10-ounce package frozen raspberries, thawed	● In a covered blender container or food processor bowl process raspberries till smooth. Strain; discard seeds.
1	6-ounce can frozen lemonade concentrate, thawed	● In a pitcher combine raspberries, lemonade concentrate, and 1 cup *water;* chill. To serve, combine raspberry mixture with carbonated beverage. Serve over *ice.* Garnish with lemon slices. Makes eight (8-ounce) servings.
1	1-liter bottle lemon-lime carbonated beverage Lemon slices	

Nutrition information per serving: 199 calories, 0 g protein, 52 g carbohydrate, 0 g fat, 0 mg cholesterol, 1 mg sodium, 80 mg potassium.

Tangy raspberries, sweet citrus, and tiny bubbles make this a wonderful refresher.

Mint Cooler

Pictured on page 65.

2	tablespoons fresh mint leaves	● In a saucepan crush mint leaves with a spoon. Add water and lemon juice. Stir in sugar. Bring to boiling; reduce heat. Simmer 5 minutes. Remove from heat. Cool; pour into pitcher. Add orange juice. Cover and chill 2 to 24 hours.
1	cup water	
¼	cup lemon juice	
¾	cup sugar	
1	cup orange juice	
1	1-liter bottle lemon-lime carbonated beverage, chilled Crushed ice Fresh mint sprigs	● To serve, remove mint leaves; add chilled carbonated beverage to juice mixture. Mix well. Fill glasses with ice. Add juice mixture; garnish with mint. Makes eight (8-ounce) servings.

Nutrition information per serving: 148 calories, 0 g protein, 38 g carbohydrate, 0 g fat, 0 mg cholesterol, 1 mg sodium, 69 mg potassium.

Here's a sophisticated nonalcoholic sipper that's a real thirst quencher!

Piña Colada Flip

Pictured on page 65.

2	cups unsweetened pineapple juice	● In a pitcher mix pineapple juice and cream of coconut. Stir in club soda.
½	cup cream of coconut	
2	cups club soda	
1	pint vanilla ice cream	● Serve in glasses. Top with ice cream. Makes four (10-ounce) servings.

Nutrition information per serving: 262 calories, 4 g protein, 36 g carbohydrate, 13 g fat, 30 mg cholesterol, 74 mg sodium, 326 mg potassium.

The pineapple and coconut in this drink conjure up images of palm trees swaying in the breeze.

Sun Tea

6 to 8 tea bags **1½ quarts cold water**	● Place tea bags in a 2-quart clear glass container. Add water; cover. Let stand in full sun or at room temperature for 2 to 3 hours or till of desired strength.
Ice **Sugar (optional)** **Lemon (optional)**	● Remove tea bags. Serve over ice. Pass sugar and lemon, if desired. Makes eight (6-ounce) servings.

Nutrition information per serving: 4 calories, 0 g protein, 1 g carbohydrate, 0 g fat, 0 mg cholesterol, 0 mg sodium, 44 mg potassium.

Have fun in the sun and brew this no-work tea at the same time!

Berry Slush

Pictured on page 65.

½ of a 6-ounce can frozen limeade *or* lemonade concentrate **⅓ cup light rum** **1½ cups fresh *or* frozen strawberries** **2 tablespoons sugar** **Ice cubes**	● In a blender container combine limeade or lemonade, and rum. Add strawberries and sugar. Blend till smooth. With blender running, add ice cubes, one at a time, through opening in lid to make 4 cups of slushy mixture. (If mixture becomes too thick before making 4 cups, add some water.)
3 strawberries, halved	● Pour or spoon into glasses. If desired, garnish with strawberries. Makes six (4-ounce) servings.

Nutrition information per serving: 82 calories, 0 g protein, 14 g carbohydrate, 0 g fat, 0 mg cholesterol, 1 mg sodium, 71 mg potassium.

This icy sipper is ideal to keep on hand for cooling off unexpected guests on hot summer days. The slush can be made up to a week ahead and frozen.

Fruity Summer Punch

Pictured on pages 4 and 5

2 cups orange juice **1 cup grapefruit juice** **⅓ cup sugar** **¼ cup lemon juice** **2 cups cracked ice** **3 cups club soda**	● In a large pitcher pour orange juice, grapefruit juice, sugar, and lemon juice over cracked ice. Add club soda.
1 medium orange, sliced	● Float orange slices in each glass. Makes eight (8-ounce) servings.

Nutrition information per serving: 109 calories, 1 g protein, 27 g carbohydrate, 0 g fat, 0 mg cholesterol, 3 mg sodium, 270 mg potassium.

This tangy fruit drink is great for punching out summer thirst.

Ice Cream Dips and Tips

On a hot summer day, nothing delights your taste buds more than scoopfuls of something cool and creamy. Dip into one of the delicious ice cream or yogurt flavors on the following pages and make your own delicious treats. To get you started, we've given some basics for using an ice cream freezer. But if you don't own one, don't despair! We've included several frozen dessert recipes you can make without one.

1 To freeze ice cream, pour the ice cream ingredients listed in the recipe into a freezer can until it is two-thirds full. Fit the can securely into the freezer bucket. Stand the dasher (paddle) up straight; cover with the lid.

4 Let the ice cream stand for 3 to 4 hours. Uncover; remove ice to below the level of the freezer lid. Wipe the can and lid to remove any salt and ice. Now, dig in!

2 Alternately pack layers of crushed ice and rock salt into the freezer bucket, using one part rock salt to six parts ice (measure by weight). Fit the handle or motor into place; secure. Follow the manufacturer's directions for freezing. Add more ice and salt as the ice melts. Remove the ice to below the can lid so no salty water seeps in.

3 Wipe the can and lid with a damp cloth to remove salt. Remove lid and dasher; scrape ice cream from the dasher back into the can. To ripen ice cream, cover can with waxed paper or foil and plug hole in lid. Cover can with lid. Next, pack additional layers of ice and salt into outer container; this time, use 4 parts ice to 1 part salt. Cover freezer with a heavy cloth or newspapers.

Vanilla Ice Cream

3 cups light cream
1½ cups sugar
1 tablespoon vanilla
3 cups whipping cream

● In a large mixing bowl combine light cream, sugar, and vanilla. Stir till sugar dissolves. Stir in whipping cream.

● Freeze in a 4- or 5-quart ice cream freezer according to manufacturer's directions. Makes 2 quarts (16 servings).

Nutrition information per serving: 313 calories, 2 g protein, 22 g carbohydrate, 25 fat, 91 mg cholesterol, 35 mg sodium, 88 mg potassium.

Maple-Walnut Ice Cream: Prepare as above, *except* decrease sugar to 1¼ cups and add 1 cup *chopped walnuts* and ½ cup *maple syrup* with the whipping cream.

Nutrition information per serving: 374 calories, 3 g protein, 26 g carbohydrate, 30 g fat, 91 mg cholesterol, 36 mg sodium, 143 mg potassium.

Cookie Ice Cream: Prepare as above, *except* add 2 cups crumbled *chocolate chip cookies* with the whipping cream.

Nutrition information per serving: 378 calories, 3 g protein, 31 g carbohydrate, 28 g fat, 96 mg cholesterol, 98 mg sodium, 93 mg potassium.

Toasting nuts really boosts their flavor. Next time you want to serve them in or on ice cream, give toasting a try and see what we mean. To toast nuts, place ½ cup of nuts in a single layer in a shallow baking pan. Bake in a 350° oven about 5 minutes or till light brown. (*Or,* place nuts in a 2-cup measure. Micro-cook on 100% power (high) for 2 to 3 minutes.)

Ice Cream and More

What could be better on homemade ice cream than homemade toppings?

Peanut Butter Topping: In a small saucepan combine ½ cup *peanut butter,* ¼ cup *light corn syrup,* 2 tablespoons *milk,* and 2 tablespoons *margarine* or *butter.* Cook and stir just until peanut butter and margarine or butter melt. Serve warm. Makes ¾ cup.

Chocolate Mallow Sauce: In a small saucepan, combine 3 (1-ounce) cut-up squares *semisweet chocolate* and ⅔ cup *light cream.* Cook and stir over medium heat until chocolate melts. Remove from heat. Stir in a 7-ounce jar *marshmallow crème* till combined. Cool and serve. Cover and store any remaining sauce in refrigerator. Stir before using. Makes about 2 cups.

Fudgy Ice Cream

2 **cups whipping cream** 3 **1-ounce squares unsweetened chocolate, chopped**	● In saucepan mix *1 cup* of the whipping cream and the chocolate over low heat till chocolate is melted. In a bowl, combine chocolate mixture and remaining whipping cream. Chill thoroughly. Beat chilled mixture till stiff peaks form. Set aside.
1 **14-ounce can sweetened condensed milk** 2 **teaspoons vanilla** 1 **cup chopped nuts, toasted**	● In a large mixing bowl combine sweetened condensed milk and vanilla. Fold in whipped cream mixture and nuts. Pour into a 9x5x3-inch loaf pan. Freeze 6 hours or till firm. Makes about 1½ quarts (12 to 16 servings).

Nutrition information per serving: 385 calories, 8 g protein, 30 g carbohydrate, 28 g fat, 69 mg cholesterol, 124 mg sodium, 339 mg potassium.

Rocky Road Ice Cream: Prepare as above, *except* fold in 2 cups *tiny marshmallows* with the nuts.

Nutrition information per serving: 410 calories, 8 g protein, 36 g carbohydrate, 28 g fat, 70 mg cholesterol, 127 mg sodium, 339 mg potassium.

Here's the scoop on this nutty, fudgy ice cream. You make it in the freezer compartment of your refrigerator, so you don't need an ice cream freezer!

Fruity Frozen Yogurt

1 **cup fresh *or* frozen whole strawberries, raspberries, *or* blueberries; sliced, peeled peaches *or* nectarines; *or* pitted dark sweet cherries** 2 **8-ounce cartons fruit-flavored yogurt** ⅓ **cup honey *or* sugar** ½ **teaspoon vanilla**	● In a covered blender container or food processor bowl blend or process fruit till smooth. Press through a sieve to remove seeds, if necessary. Stir in yogurt, honey or sugar, and vanilla. Pour into a 1- or 2-quart ice cream freezer. Freeze according to manufacturer's directions. *Or,* transfer to an 8x4x2-inch or 9x5x3-inch loaf pan; cover and freeze till firm. Break the frozen mixture into chunks; transfer to a chilled mixing bowl. Beat with an electric mixer till fluffy. Return mixture to cold pan. Cover; freeze till mixture is firm.

● Scoop into cones or bowls. Makes about 3 cups (6 servings).

Nutrition information per serving: 144 calories, 4 g protein, 32 g carbohydrate, 1 g fat, 3 mg cholesterol, 45 mg sodium, 202 mg potassium.

Match the yogurt flavor you purchase to the fruit you use and get a double wallop of flavor.

Minty Ice Cream Torte

1 10¾-ounce loaf frozen pound cake	● Cut *frozen* pound cake horizontally into 2 equal layers. Place bottom layer on a 24x12-inch piece of aluminum foil. Cut ice cream into 1-inch slices. Arrange slices side by side on the pound cake layer. Top with second cake layer. Trim cake to fit, if necessary.
1 pint brick mint ice cream*	

1 tablespoon green crème de menthe
1 4-ounce container frozen whipped dessert topping, thawed
Chocolate-mint wafers (optional)

● For frosting, fold the crème de menthe into whipped dessert topping. Spread top and sides of cake with frosting mixture. Place, uncovered, in freezer for 2 hours or till topping is frozen hard.

Remove torte from freezer. Bring ends of foil up, double-fold over top, and fold in ends. Return to freezer till ready to serve. Store up to 2 weeks in freezer.

If desired, make small chocolate curls (see tip, right). Also, cut 10 to 12 chocolate-mint wafers in half diagonally. Garnish torte with chocolate curls and wafer halves before serving. Makes 8 servings.

***Note:** If ice cream is unavailable in brick pints, buy a ½-gallon brick of ice cream and cut a 1-inch slice lengthwise. Use this large slice in place of the smaller slices above. Freeze remaining ice cream for another use.

Nutrition information per serving: 287 calories, 4 g protein, 35 g carbohydrate, 14 g fat, 88 mg cholesterol, 163 mg sodium, 100 mg potassium.

With this festive party dessert, you can have your cake—and ice cream, too! Enjoy one of our flavor combinations or make up one of your own.

Using chocolate curls to dress up this dessert makes it as beautiful as it is delicious. To make the chocolate curls, allow the chocolate-mint wafers to come to room temperature. Pressing a vegetable peeler at a slight angle to the wafer, carefully draw the edge of the peeler across long, narrow edge of the wafer. To prevent breaking the curls as you move them, insert a toothpick through the end of each curl and gently transfer them.

Butter Brickle Ice Cream Torte:
Assemble torte as above, *except* use butter brickle ice cream. For frosting, omit crème de menthe. Add 1 tablespoon *crème de cacao* and ½ cup *crushed chocolate-covered English toffee bars* or *chocolate-covered butter brickle bars* to the whipped topping. Omit layered chocolate-mint wafers.

Nutrition information per serving: 320 calories, 4 g protein, 36 g carbohydrate, 18 g fat, 87 mg cholesterol, 178 mg sodium, 107 mg potassium.

Minty Ice Cream Torte

**Tropical
Sherbet Pie**
(see recipe, page 74)

Tropical Sherbet Pie

Pictured on page 73.

2 cups flaked coconut ½ cup finely chopped nuts 3 tablespoons margarine *or* butter, melted	● In a medium mixing bowl combine coconut, nuts, and melted margarine or butter. Transfer coconut mixture to a 9-inch pie plate. Press mixture evenly onto bottom and up sides to form a firm even crust. Bake in a 325° oven about 20 minutes or till golden. Cool.
1 medium banana, sliced 1½ cups lemon sherbet, softened 1½ cups lime sherbet, softened 1½ cups orange sherbet, softened	● Evenly arrange sliced bananas over crust. Spread lemon sherbet over bananas. Top with a layer of lime sherbet, then add a layer of orange sherbet. Freeze pie 4 to 24 hours.
⅓ cup coconut, toasted 1 lime twist (optional)	● Sprinkle coconut atop. If desired, garnish with lime twist. Serves 8.

The long, hot days of summer call for the cool, light taste of this sherbet pie. Besides having a great flavor, this frozen dessert looks terrific and is easy to assemble.

Nutrition information per serving: 327 calories, 3 g protein, 38 g carbohydrate, 20 g fat, 5 mg cholesterol, 90 mg sodium, 269 mg potassium.

Frozen Fresh-Fruit Dessert

½ of an 8-ounce container soft-style cream cheese ⅓ cup sugar ¼ cup dairy sour cream ½ teaspoon finely shredded lemon peel 2 tablespoons lemon juice	● In a small mixing bowl combine cream cheese, sugar, sour cream, lemon peel, and lemon juice.
1½ cups fresh fruit (blueberries; halved seedless green grapes; pitted cherries; sliced strawberries; *or* peeled, chopped peaches, nectarines, *or* papaya)	● Fold desired fruit into cream cheese mixture. Place paper bake cups in four 6-ounce custard cups. Fill cups with fruit mixture. Freeze 4 to 24 hours.
	● To serve, remove bake cups. Place frozen desserts on plates. Let stand about 30 minutes to partially thaw. Serves 4.

Serve the kids something fun from the freezer for dessert. Freeze this refreshing fruit-and-cream mixture in flat-bottomed ice-cream cones.

Nutrition information per serving: 224 calories, 3 g protein, 26 g carbohydrate, 13 g fat, 7 mg cholesterol, 82 mg sodium, 196 mg potassium.

Cookie Cones

½ cup sugar
2 egg whites
¾ cup all-purpose flour
¼ cup margarine *or* butter,
    melted
2 tablespoons water
2 tablespoons chopped
    almonds (optional)
   Chopped almonds

● In a small bowl use an electric mixer to beat together sugar and egg whites. Add flour and beat till smooth. Slowly beat in melted margarine or butter. Stir in the water and *2 tablespoons* nuts, if desired. Grease and flour a large baking sheet. Drop about *3 tablespoons* of batter onto cookie sheet. Using a spatula or the back of a fork, spread batter into a 7-inch circle. Repeat for a second circle. If desired, sprinkle with more nuts.

● Bake cookies in a 400° oven 6 to 8 minutes or till golden. With a metal spatula or pancake turner, quickly lift off cookies, one at a time, placing each bottom-side up on a paper towel.

● Protecting your fingers with a paper towel, quickly roll one cookie into a cone and place it seam-side down on a kitchen counter until completely cool. Repeat with second cookie. (If second cookie is too cool to roll easily, return it to the oven for 1 to 2 minutes.) Repeat this baking and rolling process with remaining batter. Makes 5 or 6 cones.

Nutrition information per serving: 233 calories, 3 g protein, 34 g carbohydrate, 9 g fat, 0 mg cholesterol, 128 mg sodium, 41 mg potassium.

Here's an answer for those desserts that are so good you wish you could eat the dish, too. How? Quickly mold a hot cookie onto the bottom of a 6-ounce custard cup. After the sundae cup cools, remove the custard cup. Use the sundae cup for your favorite dessert.

Bumper Crop Fruit

On hot summer days nothing fills the dessert bill like fresh fruit. Of course, it's great as is, but if you prefer something a bit fancier, take your pick from our mouth-watering ideas.

Slice a purchased angel food cake in half horizontally to make two layers. Combine 4 cups fresh sliced fruit with 2 cups sweetened whipped cream or frozen dessert topping, thawed. Spread half of the fruit mixture on the bottom layer, top with the other layer, and add the remaining fruit mixture on the top. Refrigerate for 2 hours before serving.

Nutrition information per serving: 196 calories, 3 g protein, 30 g carbohydrate, 8 g fat, 27 mg cholesterol, 67 mg sodium, 129 mg potassium.

Spoon chunks of fresh fruit or whole berries into long-stemmed wine glasses; cover fruit with sparkling mineral water or champagne. Serve with purchased butter or sugar cookies.

Spread or pipe crackers with a purchased flavored cream cheese and arrange fruit pieces on top. Use colorful fruits, such as kiwi, strawberries, cantaloupe, honeydew or other melon, grapes, blueberries, mandarin oranges, *or* pineapple.

Slit unpeeled bananas lengthwise, cutting to, but not through the opposite side; open slightly. Grill over *medium* coals or broil 5 to 6 inches from heat until skins darken and banana softens. Let each person season his or her own banana with rum, brandy, a flavored liqueur, brown or powdered sugar, or lemon or lime wedges.

Place quarters of ripe, fresh pineapple or halves of fresh pears, apples, grapefruit, or peeled peaches, cut side up, on an unheated broiler pan. Sprinkle fruit with brown sugar; broil 5 to 6 inches from heat for 3 to 5 minutes or till warm and sugar melts. If desired, dot with margarine or butter.

Scoop out pulp from a watermelon half, being careful to keep the rind intact. If desired, cut points or scallops in rind. Cut pulp into cubes or balls. Return melon pieces to watermelon "bowl." If desired, add other fruits, such as cantaloupe or other melon, grapes, or strawberries. Add chilled white wine, fruit-flavored wine, or lemon-lime carbonated beverage just before serving.

For a mock crème brûlèe, place fruit slices or chunks, or whole berries in a broiler-proof pan. Spoon sour cream or plain yogurt over fruit and sprinkle with brown sugar. Allow 2 tablespoons sour cream or yogurt and 1 tablespoon brown sugar for each cup of fruit. Broil 5 to 6 inches from heat for 3 to 5 minutes or till sugar melts.

Nutrition information per serving:
96 calories, 1 g protein, 16 g carbohydrate, 4 g fat, 7 mg cholesterol, 11 mg sodium, 257 mg potassium.

Dip wedges of fresh pear, apple, or nectarine; orange sections; or whole strawberries in melted white or dark chocolate. Cover only half the fruit with chocolate to allow colors to show. Place on a foil-lined baking sheet and freeze 2 to 3 minutes to harden chocolate. Refrigerate dipped fruit until ready to serve. (Hint: dip fruits that will discolor, such as apples, pears, and nectarines, in lemon juice and pat dry with paper towels before dipping in chocolate.)

Make fruit kabobs using a variety of fruit chunks, whole berries, or seedless grapes. Serve with pudding or flavored yogurt. Use scooped-out grapefruit, small melon rinds, or orange-shell halves for dip containers.

Rhubarb-Berry Cobbler

¾ **cup sugar** 2 **tablespoons cornstarch** ⅓ **cup water** 3 **cups sliced fresh rhubarb** 2 **cups fresh strawberries,** **halved**	● For filling, in a medium saucepan combine sugar and cornstarch. Stir in the water; add rhubarb. Cook and stir till thickened and bubbly. Stir in strawberries; heat through. Cover and keep warm.
1 **cup all-purpose flour** ¼ **cup sugar** 1 **teaspoon baking powder** ¼ **cup margarine** *or* **butter** 1 **beaten egg** 3 **tablespoons milk** ¼ **teaspoon vanilla**	● For topping, combine flour, sugar, and baking powder. Cut in margarine or butter till mixture resembles coarse crumbs. Combine egg, milk, and vanilla. Add to flour mixture, stirring just to moisten dry ingredients.
Ice cream (optional)	● Pour hot filling into an 8x8x2-inch baking dish. Drop topping into 6 mounds atop filling. Bake in a 375° oven 20 to 25 minutes or till a toothpick inserted into topping comes out clean. Serve warm with ice cream, if desired. Makes 6 servings.

Nutrition information per serving: 332 calories, 5 g protein, 60 g carbohydrate, 9 g fat, 46 mg cholesterol, 158 mg sodium, 335 mg potassium.

If you don't have fresh rhubarb or strawberries, use the same amount of frozen fruit. There's no need to thaw it because the fruit thaws while the filling cooks.

Peach-Blueberry Crisp

4 **cups sliced, peeled fresh**
    peaches *or* **frozen sliced**
    peaches
1 **cup fresh** *or* **frozen**
    blueberries
¼ **cup sugar**
	● For filling, thaw frozen fruit, if using. Do not drain. In a 10x6-inch baking dish combine fruit and sugar. Set aside.

½ **cup packed brown sugar**
½ **cup quick-cooking rolled**
    oats
¼ **cup all-purpose flour**
1 **teaspoon finely shredded**
    lemon peel
¼ **teaspoon ground**
    cinnamon *or* **nutmeg**
¼ **cup margarine** *or* **butter**
¼ **cup coarsely chopped**
    walnuts
	● In a mixing bowl combine brown sugar, oats, flour, lemon peel, and cinnamon or nutmeg. Cut in margarine or butter till mixture resembles coarse crumbs. Stir in walnuts.
	    Sprinkle crumb mixture over filling. Bake in a 375° oven 30 to 35 minutes. (Or, if using frozen fruit, bake 40 minutes.) Serve warm. Serves 4 to 6.

Nutrition information per serving: 453 calories, 5 g protein, 75 g carbohydrate, 17 g fat, 0 mg cholesterol, 145 mg sodium, 541 mg potassium.

No flour to sift or crust to roll! That's the beauty of a crisp. It goes together in no time and tastes so good.

To save even more time, micro-cook the crisp. First, mix the filling and cover with vented, clear plastic wrap. Micro-cook on 100% power (high) 5 to 7 minutes or till fruit is tender, stirring twice. Meanwhile, prepare topping. When filling is cooked, sprinkle it with topping. Cook, uncovered, on 100% power (high) about 3 minutes or till topping is hot, giving the dish a half-turn once.

Index

A-C

Almond Chicken, 17
Antipasto Salad, 6
Apple-Chicken Salad, 44
Asparagus Salad, 43
Beans
    Bean Quartet, 63
    Easy Picnic Baked Beans, 63
    Maple Beans, 63
    Marinated Bean Salad, 60
Beef
    Beef and Fresh Tomato
        Stir-Fry, 15
    Broiled Beef, 19
    Crockery Barbecued Beef, 23
    Dilly Beef Sandwiches, 7
    Lime-Beef Salad, 46
    Mexican Pizza Pitas, 37
    Pocket Joes, 38
Berry-Glazed Picnic Cake, 53
Berry-Poppy Seed Salad, 42
Berry Slush, 67
Beverages
    Berry Slush, 67
    Fruity Summer Punch, 67
    Lemony Wine Spritzer, 64
    Make-Ahead Lemonade
        Base, 64
    Mint Cooler, 66
    Piña Colada Flip, 66
    Raspberry Sparkler, 66
    Razzle-Dazzle Lemonade, 64
    Sun Tea, 67
    Tropical Cooler, 64

Keep track of your daily nutrition needs by using the information we provide at the end of each recipe. We've analyzed the nutritional content of each recipe serving for you. When a recipe gives an ingredient substitution, we used the first choice in the analysis. And if it makes a range of servings (such as 4 to 6), we used the smallest number. Ingredients listed as optional weren't included in the calculations.

Blue Cheese Butter, 29
Broiled Beef, 19
Butter Brickle Ice Cream Torte, 72
Cajun Butter, 29
Cantaloupe-Chicken Salad, 47
Cashew Chicken Stir-Fry, 17
Cheddar-Jalapeño Spread, 29
Cheese-Sauced Vegetables, 25
Cheesy Grilled Potatoes, 30
Chicken
    Almond Chicken, 17
    Apple-Chicken Salad, 44
    Cantaloupe-Chicken Salad, 47
    Cashew Chicken Stir-Fry, 17
    Chicken Marsala with
        Mushrooms, 8
    Chicken Pecan Roll-Ups, 34
    Curried Fruity Chicken Salad, 46
    Herbed Chicken, 51
    Layered Tortilla Sandwich, 33
    Polynesian Chicken Sandwich, 35
    Walnut Chicken, 17
Chive-Roasted Corn, 31
Chocolate Mallow Sauce, 70
Coleslaw, 61
Cookie Cones, 75
Cookie Ice Cream, 70
Crab-Stuffed Lobster Tails, 18
Curried Fruity Chicken Salad, 46
Curried Pineapple-Orange Salad, 43

D-L

Desserts
    Berry-Glazed Picnic Cake, 53
    Butter Brickle Ice Cream Torte, 72
    Chocolate Mallow Sauce, 70
    Cookie Cones, 75
    Cookie Ice Cream, 70
    Frozen Fresh Fruit Dessert, 74
    Fruity Frozen Yogurt, 71
    Fudgy Ice Cream, 71
    Maple Walnut Ice Cream, 70
    Minty Ice Cream Torte, 72
    No-Bake Fruit Pie, 7
    Nut-Topped Snack Cake, 61
    Peach-Blueberry Crisp, 78
    Peanut Butter Topping, 70
    Rhubarb-Berry Cobbler, 78
    Rocky Road Ice Cream, 71

Desserts (continued)
    Tropical Sherbet Pie, 74
    Vanilla Ice Cream, 70
Deviled Eggs, 55
Dilly Beef Sandwiches, 7
Easy-Does-It Potato Salad, 59
Easy Picnic Baked Beans, 63
Eggs, Deviled, 55
Fennel Butter, 29
Fish and Seafood
    Crab-Stuffed Lobster Tails, 18
    Fish Steaks with Zucchini
        Mayonnaise, 12
    Fish with Tarragon, 19
    Marinated Shrimp Salad, 42
    Mariner's Garden Chowder, 22
    Seafood Skillet Stir-Fry, 11
    Swordfish Kabobs, 20
Frozen Fresh Fruit Dessert, 74
Fruity Frozen Yogurt, 71
Fruity Summer Punch, 67
Fudgy Ice Cream, 71
Garlic Spread, 29
Grilling Recipes
    Cheesy Grilled Potatoes, 30
    Chive-Roasted Corn, 31
    Crab-Stuffed Lobster Tails, 18
    Fish with Tarragon, 19
    Swordfish Kabobs, 20
    Zucchini-Tomato Grill, 30
Ham Sandwiches with Apricot
    Mustard, 38
Herbed Chicken, 51
Herbed Cottage Cheese Salad, 47
Hoagie Pocket, 37
Homemade Pesto, 52
Hot Mustard Potato Salad, 57
Ice Cream
    Butter Brickle Ice Cream Torte, 72
    Cookie Ice Cream, 70
    Fudgy Ice Cream, 71
    Maple Walnut Ice Cream, 70
    Minty Ice Cream Torte, 72
    Rocky Road Ice Cream, 71
    Vanilla Ice Cream, 70
Icy Salsa Garden Soup, 25
Italian Herb Spread, 29
Italian-Style Picnic Sandwich, 34
Layered Tortilla Sandwich, 33

Lemon-Basil Butter, 29
Lemon-Herb Buttered
    Vegetables, 25
Lemony Wine Spritzer, 64
Lime-Beef Salad, 46
Linguine with Zucchini and
    Kielbasa, 10
Lobster Tails, Crab-Stuffed, 18

M-R

Make-Ahead Lemonade
    Base, 64
Maple Beans, 63
Maple Walnut Ice Cream, 70
Marinated Bean Salad, 60
Marinated Shrimp Salad, 42
Mariner's Garden Chowder, 22
Medley Salad, 51
Mexican Pizza Pitas, 37
Microwave Recipes
    Mexican Pizza Pitas, 37
    Pocket Joes, 38
    Polynesian Chicken Sandwich, 35
    Seafood Skillet Stir-Fry, 11
Mint Cooler, 66
Minty Ice Cream Torte, 72
New Red Potato Salad, 58
No-Bake Fruit Pie, 7
Nut-Topped Snack Cake, 61
Orange-Sauced Pork Chops, 13
Parmesan Butter, 29
Peach-Blueberry Crisp, 78
Peanut Butter Topping, 70
Piña Colada Flip, 66
Pocket Joes, 38
Polynesian Chicken Sandwich, 35
Pork
    Orange-Sauced Pork Chops, 13
    Sausage-Pepper Hoagies, 39
    Stir-Fried Pork in Hoisin Sauce, 16
Potato Salads
    Easy-Does-It Potato Salad, 59
    Hot Mustard Potato Salad, 57
    New Red Potato Salad, 58
    Traditional Potato Salad, 56
    Vinaigrette Potato Salad, 57
Potatoes, Cheesy Grilled, 30
Primavera Salad, 52
Raspberry Sparkler, 66

Razzle-Dazzle Lemonade, 64
Rhubarb-Berry Cobbler, 78
Rocky Road Ice Cream, 71

S-Z

Salads
    Antipasto Salad, 6
    Apple-Chicken Salad, 44
    Asparagus Salad, 43
    Berry-Poppy Seed Salad, 42
    Cantaloupe-Chicken Salad, 47
    Coleslaw, 61
    Curried Fruity Chicken Salad, 46
    Curried Pineapple-Orange
        Salad, 43
    Easy-Does-It Potato Salad, 59
    Herbed Cottage Cheese Salad, 47
    Hot Mustard Potato Salad, 57
    Lime-Beef Salad, 46
    Marinated Bean Salad, 60
    Marinated Shrimp Salad, 42
    Medley Salad, 51
    New Red Potato Salad, 58
    Primavera Salad, 52
    Traditional Potato Salad, 56
    Vinaigrette Potato Salad, 57
Sandwiches
    Chicken Pecan Roll-Ups, 34
    Dilly Beef Sandwiches, 7
    Ham Sandwiches with Apricot
        Mustard, 38
    Hoagie Pocket, 37
    Italian-Style Picnic Sandwich, 34
    Layered Tortilla Sandwich, 33
    Mexican Pizza Pitas, 37
    Pocket Joes, 38
    Polynesian Chicken Sandwich, 35
    Sausage-Pepper Hoagies, 39
    Veggiewiches, 39
Saucy Kielbasa, 10
Sausage-Pepper Hoagies, 39
Seafood Skillet Stir-Fry, 11
Shrimp Salad, Marinated, 42
Stir-Fried Pork in Hoisin Sauce, 16
Sun Tea, 67
Swordfish Kabobs, 20
Tarragon-Onion Spread, 29
Traditional Potato Salad, 56
Tropical Cooler, 64

Tropical Sherbet Pie, 74
Vanilla Ice Cream, 70
Vegetables
    Antipasto Salad, 6
    Asparagus Salad, 43
    Bean Quartet, 63
    Cheese-Sauced Vegetables, 25
    Cheesy Grilled Potatoes, 30
    Chive-Roasted Corn, 31
    Easy Picnic Baked Beans, 63
    Icy Salsa Garden Soup, 25
    Lemon-Herb Buttered
        Vegetables, 25
    Maple Beans, 63
    Marinated Bean Salad, 60
    Medley Salad, 51
    Primavera Salad, 52
    Vegetables with Nuts, 25
    Veggiewiches, 39
    Zucchini-Tomato Grill, 30
Veggiewiches, 39
Vinaigrette Potato Salad, 57
Walnut Chicken, 17
Zucchini-Tomato Grill, 30

Tips

Feeding the Gang, 60
Grilling Charts, 26-28
Homemade Pesto, 52
How Hot Is It?, 31
Ice Cream and More, 70
Keep the Lid On It!, 22
One Potato, Two Potato, 58
Picnic Pointers, 54
Quick and Easy Cooked Chicken, 33
Quick-Fix Main Dishes, 10
Steak Doneness, 28
Stir-Frying Tips, 16